The Throws Manual

George D. Dunn, Jr. and Kevin McGill

2nd Edition

TAFNEWS PRESS

Book Division of Track & Field News

SECOND EDITION

Published by Tafnews Press,
Book Division of Track & Field News,
2570 El Camino Real, Suite 606,
Mountain View, CA 94040 USA.

First edition copyrighted in 1991.
Second edition, first printing, 1994
Second edition, second printing, 2000

Standard Book Number 0-911521-39-9

Printed in the United States of America

Cover design and production by Teresa Tam
Drawings by Teresa Tam

CONTENTS

DEDICATION

I am truly indebted to my wife Carolyn for the hours she spent proofreading my contributions to this manual and to all my conference and state champions and those athletes who may not have achieved the gold but paid the price as much as those who did. In addition, I am grateful to my daughter, Lynette, who was one of my "athletes" and is a continual source of encouragement and help through track discussions and active coaching assistance.

George Dunn, Jr.

To two of the greatest minds in throwing: Tom McDermott and Bob Sing. Both have been missionaries for their events, Tom in the hammer, and Bob in the javelin. Hundreds of coaches and athletes owe their thanks to these men. Cheers to both!!!!

Kevin McGill

PHOTOGRAPHER CREDITS

Page	Athlete	Photographer
Cover	Karl Salb	Rich Clarkson
17	Randy Matson	
24	John Godina	Chai von der Laage / The Sporting Image
41	Randy Barnes	ALLSPORT / Mike Powell
46	Valentina Fedyushina	ALLSPORT / Gray Mortimore
49	Astrid Kumbernuss	Chai von der Laage / The Sporting Image
51	Dave Laut	Jeff Johnson / Geek Media
53	Al Oerter	Rich Clarkson
58	Jürgen Schult	*Los Angeles Times*
66	Lars Riedel	ALLSPORT / Mike Powell
71	Yuriy Syedikh	ALLSPORT / Michael King
75	Dawn Ellerbe	Claus Anderson / The Sporting Image
80	Lance Deal	John Giustina
81	Hal Connolly	Fionnbar Callanan
88	Balázs Kiss	Bill Leung, Jr. / Geek Media
101	Petra Felke	ALLSPORT / Gray Mortimore
106	Jan Zelezny	ALLSPORT / Gray Mortimore
109	Tom Petranoff	Jeff Johnson / Geek Media
113	Trine Hattestad	ALLSPORT / Mike Powell
114	Tom Pukstys	John Giustina
120	Natalya Shikolenko	ALLSPORT / Mike Powell

PREFACE

While researching for this book, the authors were unable to find a comprehensive manual on the throws. Outside of Bob Sing's excellent javelin book, nothing has been published in recent years which attempts to cover all of the aspects of teaching and coaching the throws. This provided us the incentive to rectify this.

We have covered all four throws in this book, despite the sad fact that the javelin and especially the hammer have not grown to the status of the shot and discus in the USA. Our hope is that this book will encourage many shot/discus coaches to learn and introduce the javelin and hammer in their areas.

Angel Spassov, a Bulgarian weightlifting coach, has said that, in Eastern Europe, coaches know each other and openly exchange training ideas, technical points, etc. The lack of material on throwing in the USA has led to the exact opposite scenario. We suffer in the throws because our coaches guard their material as if it were secret information. This lack of exchange prevents feedback from fine-tuning certain ideas which could lead to improvement. We offer this material to the coaches with the hope that we will get feedback, and that more sharing will occur in the future.

In the attempt to increase sharing and improve scientific knowledge, USA Track & Field founded the Coaching Education program. Readers interested in furthering their knowledge of throwing should investigate the Level I and II schools, which are crucial to the future of track and field in this country.

As we flounder in the age of scrutiny to prevent illegal drug use, the next generation of throws experts will be masters of periodization, training theory, psychology, and biomechanics. We hope this book will inspire you to hone your skills in these areas, which will be of great benefit to your future throwers.

With 60 years of experience between us, the authors do not proclaim to have the final word on every aspect. However, the combination of experience in high school and collegiate Divisions I and II has given us a range of vision on what may or may not be important for a throws coach. The old cliche, KISS (Keep It Simple, Stupid), is where it was, and is. You may develop the finest technical eye in the land, but if you cannot prescribe a correction for an error, you have wasted your time, and the athlete's. As you read beyond this book, we have a short piece of advice: remember your audience.

We wish you well, and much success. As the Danish hammer coach, Bjarke Dons, signs his letters, we sign off,

With my hand in my glove,

George Dunn

Kevin McGill

June, 1994

BASIC THROWING PRINCIPLES

INTRODUCTION

While there have been many pedantic biomechanical reports published in the track literature, the overall impact on the throws has been minimal. Dr. Stanley Plagenhoef summarized it best in his article, "Coaches—Get Back on the Pedestal. You Are Still Number One." That article, which appeared in the 1981 *Track and Field Quarterly Review* (Vol. 81, No. 1, p. 16), points up that the throws coach must be careful when reviewing questionable data.

Rather than concentrating on how to understand data derived from world class throwers with flawed technique, throws coaches would be better off studying Dyson and Ecker (see Suggested Readings, p. 14), to improve their understanding of the *basic* biomechanical principles in throwing. Researchers should concentrate more on how to link their findings with the working coach, or else their studies will be empty exercises.

SIX BASIC PRINCIPLES

1. Involve the whole body. This first principle sums it all up! You have to use your whole body. Not just your arm. Not just your left leg. We mean all the body parts and levers. A shot or discus thrower who fails to pivot in the center of the ring has just shut down his main power supply—the right leg. In the javelin, many beginners let the left arm hang normally at the side. Use the left arm too!

This principle applies not just to competition, but to training, too. Train the whole body. As a coach on the field, you will be looking at a body in motion. Remember: coach the whole body. Illustration #1 demonstrates this point.

In the shot put, Al Feuerbach (1) made the most of his relatively small size. This shot effort at the delivery clearly shows how he is using just about all the muscles in his body at this point to deliver the shot. Any mistake here and his throw would lose considerable distance. He has punched that right side around into a terrific block on the left side.

1

2

In the hammer (2), the thrower must control his upper body, and concentrate on using the lower body. If the athlete pulls in here, the throw can be written off. Learning to use the whole body means learning to control which part is active and which is more passive. The hammer thrower is unlike the shot putter in that, in the hammer, there is no place for using the arms in any form of extension. They are held straight as soon as the turns begin.

2. Achieve a summation of forces. Each lever we use in a throw must move faster than the previous lever, and each lever must be capable of moving faster in the direction of the throw than the implement (Dyson).

We use the stronger, larger, but slower muscles first, i.e., the thighs, trunk; the weaker, smaller, but faster muscles last, i.e. the arms, hands, feet, and lower leg. Although there is a sequence involved, it is imperative that all forces be applied as simultaneously as possible. We have all seen the young shot putter hit the center of the ring and come to a dead halt—goodbye, summation of forces.

This concept may be difficult to understand at first. It is the heart of correct technical execution, however. In the beginning, you will teach the athlete certain parts of the throw. Your success as a shot put coach, for instance, will depend on how you teach the athlete to blend the glide with the power position to produce an effective throw. Each event chapter will deal with this in more detail by using a teaching progression.

3

The javelin thrower in this illustration (3) has achieved near perfection because the large muscle groups have done their work and have left the arm behind. This stretch-pull will create a tremendous arm speed, far greater than in the run, as the thrower's arm literally whips forward due to the correct action of the lower body.

If you stop in the throw, usually due to a poor placement of the right foot, you lose momentum and have to rely more on arm power to create release velocity. In the javelin and discus, you can see the arm "drag" behind the thrower, as the lower body first does its job.

3. Apply force in the direction of the throw. 1988 Olympic champion Ulf Timmermann's success is due in great part to his ability to drive the shot from a low position at the start of the throw almost along a track directly in line with his release angle. From the side we would see a line going up into the throw. See Figure 5, line (d), on the next page. Timmermann's execution is a perfect example of applying force correctly in the direction of the throw.

Generally, the preliminary movements provide more horizontal drive than lift; in the delivery, there is more lift than drive. Timmermann has mastered the perfect balance between the two, getting terrific drive without much lift in the very beginning, then managing to stay down in position and lift at the correct time.

Along with this concept, we should note some release angles, as they indicate a general direction to actually throw:

35-41 degrees	—	shot
39 degrees	—	discus
27-34 degrees	—	"old" javelin
35-41 degrees	—	"new" javelin
42-43 degrees	—	hammer

By suggesting these angles, we do not imply that you can teach an athlete to throw exactly at any of them, or measure them accurately without fairly expensive equipment. You have to develop a feel for the correct angle, and work on teaching the proper technique. The release angle will be a result of proper technique.

In this first drawing (4) by Czech authority Klement Kerssenbrock, we can see the overhead view of the shot path for former world record holder Aleksandr Barishnikov of the USSR (rotation style). We have removed all of the other detail from the drawing, except the path of the shot.

Wait a minute! Look in the center of the ring—the shot actually goes backwards during the rotation of the body to achieve position. This really hindered Barishnikov.

Dave Laut, former American record holder, was studied in a 1983 biomechanics film, and his path was shown to be different. Dave got through the ring and moved the shot in a curved line, but not one which went *away* from the direction of the throw. Dave worked his shot into the direction of the throw, in a manner preferable to Barishnikov. This was an important advance for the rotational shot.

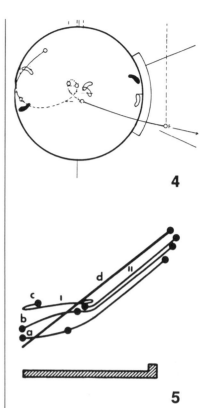

4

5

The second drawing (5), by German coach Peter Tschiene, shows the path from the side for three putters: a) Ilona Slupianek (GDR), 1980 Olympic champion, b) Udo Beyer (GDR), 1976 Olympic champion, c) Aleksandr Barishnikov (USSR), 1976 Olympic bronze medalist, and d) an optimal path, which is almost identical to the path traced in the technique of 1988 Olympic champion Ulf Timmermann (GDR).

The optimal path is the lowest line, and it goes in a steadily ascending path until release. Studies of Timmermann show that he is consistently very close to this ideal.

Barishnikov's (rotational) path starts at the highest point, a distinct disadvantage which he once tried to eliminate by literally crouching down at the start. He abandoned this attempt!

What the straight line/Timmermann path shows is that the thrower who can apply force in the direction of the throw (over the longest range of motion—see #4) will be the most effective thrower, all things being equal.

We have here three East German glide throwers (Slupianek, Beyer, Timmermann) and three different paths. Beyer did dominate the event for a while, but he never achieved the technical perfection Timmermann did, and this examination of the shot path shows why Beyer fell short of the ideal.

4. Achieve a long range of motion. During the throw, the discus thrower may have the discus up off his hip, behind him, with the arm straight. When the left foot lands in the power position, he must have placed the discus up off the line of his shoulders. The discus has in effect been raised to achieve a long range of motion.

In the hammer the thrower must learn to keep his arms straight in the turns. Unless he plants his right foot down "early" after the hammer passes 180°, he will fail to achieve a long range of motion, even with straight arms.

As you can see with the hammer, the thrower can lose his advantage unless he gets both feet into the throwing position quickly. The athlete can then exert force over a greater distance. It is imperative to remember that the greatest amount of force is applied only when both feet are on the ground.

Shot putters such as former world record holder Al Feuerbach tried to gain a greater range by twisting at the start of the preliminary movements. Since the shot would achieve its greatest velocity only in the double support system and when force is exerted in the throwing direction, it can be concluded that this experiment was not the reason for Feuerbach's great throwing. In a similar fashion, one can analyze the wrap-style in the javelin.

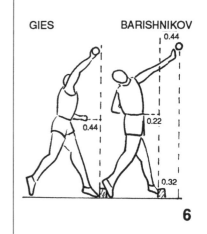

6

This drawing (6) shows the difference between two throwers, Hans-Peter Gies (GDR) and Barishnikov, at release. While Barishnikov did achieve a longer range of motion here, there are some problems. Look at his left side—there is a poor block, and his head is facing to the side. Gies was one of the great exponents of the East German short-long technique, which emphasized a short glide, on the theory that the resulting glide would put the feet on the ground sooner, thereby achieving the long range of motion in double support, our goal in all throwing events.

By sacrificing the range of motion at the board and gaining more range on the shot due to an earlier application of force, it would seem that, in this comparison, Barishnikov would lose.

The lesson we can learn from this is that we do not want to sacrifice one aspect of technique to try and gain an advantage elsewhere. In sum, the athlete may lose distance while trying to achieve something which will have marginal effect.

7

In the javelin there have been three great American contributions to the study of range of motion. The first was Bud Held (7). Aspects of this technique are not popular today, but let's see how this athlete in the early 1950's managed to throw so far.

If the picture 7 is correct in showing his left leg on the ground, there is no quesiton this is the most radical position ever achieved in the javelin. This is range of motion to the utmost.

Al Cantello in the late 1950's set a world record of 282'3$^1/_2$", using a delivery action rarely seen then or now—he flew through the air after release and landed on his hands! This acrobatic act was on the opposite side of the fence from Held. Cantello was able to hold the javelin longer in his hand and still manage to apply force.

A subsequent contribution was that of Tom Petranoff, who set the world record in 1983. Petranoff mastered the wrap or rotational method in the javelin, putting some of the Held technique together with Finnish technique, thereby achieving impressive results.

5. Weight transfer. The bodyweight is transfered from the rear leg to the front leg in the shot, discus, and javelin. In these three events, the power position involves torque when the weight is on the rear leg. At that instant, the upper body should "trail" the lower body. We may say that the hips are "open," and the shoulders are "closed."

As the weight begins to transfer, there is a simultaneous unwinding of the upper body. So, while the bodyweight is moving in the direction of the throw, the upper body comes around to face the same direction.

Just at this moment, when the upper body almost faces the throwing direction, and the weight is moving onto the front leg, a block, or stopping action on the left side occurs. There is a conscious effort to stop the left side from rotating further, consequently achieving an acceleration of the right side, which is holding the implement. In Europe, there has been such an emphasis on blocking that discus throwers do not reverse their feet in the delivery.

Sergey Litvinov once described the block in the hammer as if the hammer were a passenger in a car, without a seatbelt. The car smashes into a solid brick wall, and you know the result! The passenger/hammer continues to fly forward through the windshield.

In this illustration (8) the discus thrower is off the ground, but he has already transfered his weight properly and the terrific extension of the legs has caused this effect.

8

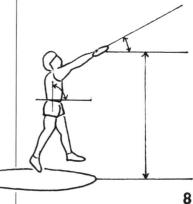

Here we see a shot putter at the moment when the block of the left leg is really taking effect (9). The weight transfer is well under way, especially since the right side is "free" to rotate around that block. The transfer will take place in a split second, enabling the thrower to use his mass to accelerate the shot put.

9

6. Center of gravity over base. During the application of force, the athlete has to have his feet in the correct position, and achieve a BALANCE. Balance problems start right at the beginning of the throw. It certainly will take some time to master this with a young thrower.

The feet are offset, right heel in line with the left toe in the power position. Now . . . you can still be off balance, depending on your prior actions. The left foot "in the bucket" problem means that the left foot is too far left. The opposite position, left leg off to right side, creates a blocked hip, which is not desirable.

The shot putter illustration (9) also shows this well, as everything comes together in the put.

In Figure 10 we see a hammer thrower with his weight perfectly balanced while in the middle of the delivery. Because he is balanced, he is able to apply the maximum force his body can generate into the throw, and isn't this our goal?

10

BASIC THROWING PRINCIPLES REFERENCES
AND SUGGESTED READING

1. Borgström, Anders. "Two Years with the new Javelin," *New Studies in Athletics,* Vol. 3, #1, 1988, pp. 85-88.

2. Doherty, Ken. *Modern Track and Field.* Englewood Cliffs: Prentice Hall, 1963. (OP)

3. Doherty, Ken. *Track & Field Omnibook.* 4th edition. Los Altos: Tafnews Press, 1985. (OP)

4. Dyson, Geoffrey, *Dyson's Mechanics of Athletics.* London: Hodder and Stoughton, 1987. (OP)

5. Ecker, Tom, *Basic Track & Field Biomechanics.* Mountain View: Tafnews Press, 1996 (2nd ed.). Available from Track & Field News, $17.50.

6. Fleuridas, Claude, et al. *Les Lancers.* Paris: Vigot, 1982.

7. Jarver, Jess, editor. *The Throws: Contempary Theory, Technique and Training.* 4th edition. Mountain View, CA: Tafnews Press, 1994. Available from Track & Field News, $16.50.

8. Kerssenbrock, Klement. "Analysis of Rotation Technique," *The Throws.* Los Altos: Tafnews Press, 1974 edition, pp. 39-41.

9. Payne, Howard. *The Science of Track and Field Athletics.* London: Pelham Books, 1981. (OP)

10. Plagenhoef, Stanley, 1981. "Coaches Get Back on the Pedestal. You Are Still Number One," *Track and Field Quarterly Review,* Vol. 81, #1, pp. 16-18.

11. Poprawski, Bogdan. "Discus and the Wind," *The Thrower.* #47, p. 25.

12. Roy, Jacques. "Le Marteau," *Revue de l'AEFA* #75, 1981, pp. 36-53.

13. Terauds, Juris. *Biomechanics of the Javelin Throw.* Del Mar: Academic Publishers, 1985. (OP)

14. Tschiene, Peter. "Shot," *Athletes in Action.* Howard Payne, ed. London: Pelham Books, 1985, pp. 198-211. (OP)

OTHER REFERENCE MATERIAL

Magazines

Track and Field News, 2570 El Camino Real, Suite 606, Mountain View, CA 94040. $38.95/year USA. This is needed for keeping up-to-date in the sport.

Track Coach (Formerly "Track Technique"), same address as above. $20/year. The complete technique journal for track and field. A good percentage of articles are on the throws. Official USATF technique quarterly.

Track and Field Coaches Review, 1406 N.W. 6th St., Suite C, Gainesville, FL 32601. $20/year. This is the U.S. Track Coaches Assn. journal.

The Thrower, c/o Max Jones, 152 Longdon Road, Knowle, Solihull B93 9HU West Midlands, England. This is the best magazine in the world which is dedicated completely to all four throws. Highest rating!

Track and Field Journal, Canadian Track and Field Association, 1600 James Naismith Drive, Gloucester, Ontario, Canada K1B 5N4. On occasion, they have had superb material, but the magazine's publication schedule can be erratic.

Sport, from same address in Canada. They have published some terrific material on strength development in the past. Generally not specific to throwing, but great on medicine, sport psychology, etc.

Modern Athlete and Coach, 1 Fox Avenue, Athelstone, S.A. 5076, Australia. $21 U.S./year. This is Jess Jarver's periodical. One of the best track journals in the world over the years!

New Studies in Athletics, IAAF Publications Dept., 17 Rue Princesse Florestine, Monte Carlo 98000, Monaco. This publication is very high quality, with glossy paper and color pictures, but has an unpredictable publication schedule. Get all the back issues.

National Strength and Conditioning Journal, Box 81410, Lincoln, NE 68501. Memberships available, which entitle you to this one, and the next journal listed, at an additional charge. This periodical has grown in stature over the years. It is now a must for those interested in strength and conditioning.

The Journal of Applied Sport Science Research, same address as above. Available with NSCA membership only. For the research-minded.

Videos

There are two recommended sources:

Dr. Lyle Knudson, c/o Development Science Projects, P.O. Box 101074, Denver, CO 80250-1074. For just $15-20 each, you can obtain videos of throwers (and other events) in actual competition from the 1990 Goodwill Games, 1990 TAC Sr. and Jr. Championships, 1989 TAC Sr. & Jr. Championships, 1989 NCAA Championships, and 1988 Olympic Trials. Also IAF biomechanics studies, 1984 Olympic Games, and more recently produced event instruction tapes put out by USATF. Excellent and very useful. Write for information and order blanks.

Track & Field News, 2570 El Camino Real, Suite 606, Mountain View, CA 94040 carries several videos on throwing, including coaching video series from Bill Dellinger, World Class (Buncic, Backes). Write for information.

SHOT PUT

Randy Matson

SHOT PUT

This chapter will give an overview of the two most common styles of shot put technique used today.

Each style has its proponents who feel that "their" style meets all the biomechanical principles necessary to obtain maximum results. In the final analysis, neither style has a monopoly on the world record. While Randy Barnes, who broke the world record in 1990, employs the rotation or spin technique, a majority of the top contemporary throwers use the more conventional glide. In fact, even though a spinner holds the world record at this writing, the recent Olympics and World Championships have been won by gliders.

What must be kept in mind is that the source of all success in the throwing events is a combination of explosive power and speed. Without it, no style will make a champion. All things being equal (size, speed, power, etc.), the athlete who utilizes the best biomechanical principles on "that given day" will be the winner.

No matter what style is used, the distance of the throw depends upon three important biomechanical principles: the angle of release, the height of release, and, most important, the speed of release.

So, an athlete interested in first-class performance must continually attempt to increase the speed of the implement. Two factors will influence implement speed: (1) muscular power and strength and (2) the length of the acceleration path.

Obviously, the stronger the athlete, the better he can come out of the low position at the back of the circle and apply maximum force against the shot. In the glide, techniquewise, the path of the shot during acceleration must be as straight as possible when observed from above and from the side.

In the opinion of the author, the athlete who has demonstrated in recent years the "ideal" model of the glide technique is Ulf Timmermann, the former world record holder and Olympic Champion from the former East Germany.

THE GLIDE TECHNIQUE

STARTING POSITION

The following instructions are for a right-handed athlete. The shot is held in the hand, resting on the base of the fingers. The three middle fingers are slightly splayed, while the thumb and little finger give lateral support.

The shot is raised over the head in the right hand, with the wrist bent so the palm of the hand faces upward. This is how the novice thrower learns to "cock" the wrist. (1)

Next, the shot is lowered until it rests against the neck under the jaw so that the thumb touches the collarbone. The elbow is raised until the upper arm forms a 80- to 90-degree angle between it and the trunk.

The athlete stands erect in the back of the circle with his back facing the stopboard, with his weight on the right foot, while the left foot is approximately 12 inches behind the right foot and about six to eight inches to the side. The left arm is relaxed (2).

19

The trunk is bent forward until the back is parallel to the circle, while at the same time, the body is lowered on the right leg until there is approximately a 30- to 40-degree angle between the trunk and the right thigh.

The left foot slides across the circle with the toes tapping the surface for balance. The eyes are focused on the rim of the circle and the left arm hangs loosely from a relaxed shoulder. To help keep the left arm and shoulder relaxed, the athlete shakes and wiggles the fingers during the time that the left arm hangs loosely from the shoulder. The right forearm is parallel to the circle and the hand is holding the shot firmly against the neck (3).

The left knee is pulled forward until it is beside the right knee which is bending even deeper so that the body is now in a compact, crouched position (3).

The hips are unseated or over-balanced toward the stopboard, while, at the same time, the left leg is swept aggressively across the circle to help initiate the drive to the front of the circle. The right leg pushes the whole body unit backward in the direction of the stopboard. The left leg stays close to the surface of the circle to prevent it from raising above hip level, thus resulting in a late landing (4).

This process should be smooth, with no jerking movement of the trunk or left arm backward and/or upward. The shoulders remain square to the back of the circle and the eyes still focus on the rim. While the angle between the trunk and the thigh remains small, there will be a natural increase of about 15 to 20 degrees (4).

The heel of the right foot is the last to leave the back of the circle. The right foot begins to rotate to the left so that when it plants in the center of the circle, it is facing the four or five o'clock position. As the right heel is still in contact with the circle and the toes are pointing upward, there is a very wide split between the legs as the left foot is reaching for the stopboard (4).

To get into the power position, the right foot must be pulled or "sucked" back under the body so that it plants near the center of the circle (5).

THE POWER POSITION

The purpose of the glide is to develop maximum momentum or kinetic energy that will be transferred to the shot. There must be very little delay between the glide and the power position and the putting phase.

If the glide is executed smoothly, the transition between the two phases is very fluid. This results only if the right foot is drawn forcefully from the back of the circle and lands on the ball of the foot in the back half or near the center of the circle, depending on the height of the athlete. Almost simultaneously, with very little delay, the left foot is planted against the stopboard in a toe-to-heel alignment—with the left toe in line with the right heel. The left foot is against the stopboard on the foot's inner edge, pointing more or less to the two o'clock position.

The shoulders are square to the rear, and the head and eyes still face toward and focus on the rim. The right forearm remains parallel to the ground and the shot is over or slightly outside the right foot. The left arm can either be pointing to the rear of the circle or out to the side as long as the shoulders still remain square to the rear and the shot stays over the

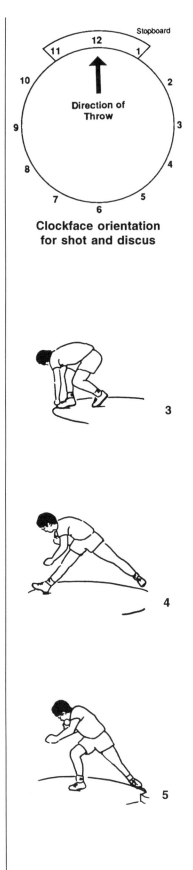

Clockface orientation for shot and discus

right foot.

The trunk must be in a good, lay-back position of 60 to 70 degrees. Anything more than that will drastically reduce the distance the athlete can lift the shot. This is a split-second position, because as soon as the right foot plants, the center of gravity (c.g.) passes over the right leg onto the left (6). This is a beneficial effect since it allows full use of the right leg.

The placement of the right foot is not universally agreed upon, but to have the longest acceleration path possible, it becomes necessary for an athlete who is over six feet tall to have the right foot in the back half of the circle. All the leading throwers of the world, and this includes both men and women, have their right foot at least three to six inches in the back half of the circle. Obviously, this requires great strength, but to be a good shot putter, the athlete must spend a great deal of time developing powerful and explosive legs.

THE PUT

It is critical at this time that the athlete think of "lifting" the shot straight up, attempting to keep the shot in a straight line through the acceleration path. The coach, when looking at the athlete from behind, should see very little deviation in the path of the shot. A coaching cue is to tell the athlete to lift with the back first, before he thinks of rotating the right shoulder to the front (7). In fact, if the athlete concentrates on the lifting action, there is no need to think of any shoulder rotation, because the rotation will be a natural reaction when he puts the shot.

The job of the right leg is to push the hips to the front. The right leg drives explosively from the toes. As it drives forward, the heel turns out and the knee turns in so that it faces down as the right hip is pushed to the front.

Because of the wide base of the power position, there is a longer increase in the acceleration path that the shot will travel when the athlete applies muscular force, especially by the legs at this time. If the athlete drives the body upward rather than pushing the hips forward, this will shorten the distance in which he can apply this muscular force.

The right shoulder and shot must remain over the right foot and leg as they are lifted straight up, while the left arm is *not* swept wide, but is led to the top by the elbow. This puts the chest in a pre-stretched position (7)(8).

With the chest pre-stretched, the oblique and lateral rotators are wound up like giant springs, ready to move the right shoulder explosively forward. Once the left shoulder and arm have reached the open position, they lead the right shoulder upward and forward. It is here that many novices will drop or drive the left shoulder down and away from the direction of the put. Be alert to this problem.

After the left elbow points upward in the direction of the put, it is pulled back and stopped abruptly at shoulder level with the arm almost parallel to the ground. The sudden stop of the fast-moving left arm causes the right shoulder to accelerate. At the same time, the chest is driven up to meet the shortening left arm.

If the athlete is told to "drive the chest to the arm," this helps to prevent the athlete from rotating the hips and chest while "sitting back" over the right leg, instead of getting up on top of the left leg at the moment of the right arm strike. This left arm action helps to set up the blocking of the left side (9)(10).

6

7

8

9

10

The left foot is slammed against the stopboard and is actually used somewhat like the planted pole of the pole vault. With the left leg acting as the pole, the tremendous block produced by the board and the left foot and leg results in a explosive lifting of the back and the right leg driving the hips to the front so that the shot is lifted up and over the top with tremendous acceleration of the upper body.

This obviously requires great leg strength, but it is very effective when properly applied and timed. It produces a braking action that transfers the kinetic energy produced in the lower extremeities to the upper body, which results in the hips being behind the left foot, rather than above the left foot (17).

To repeat important points in the whole action: the head and eyes are locked on the rim, the shot is under the chin, the elbow is high—maintaining the 90-degree angle between the arm and the trunk. As the shot moves forward and the right shoulder is rotating to the front after the initial back lift, the eyes continue looking backward until they are ripped off the rim and are then swept skyward until they face the direction of the throw.

11

12

THE EXPLOSIVE STRIKE

The arm must stay behind the shot with the elbow high during the explosive strike of the arm. The strike is a high punching action of the arm and shoulder. The hand faces backward with the thumb down and little finger up. A final impetus is added beyond the stopboard with a wrist and finger "flick." This can add as much as one to two feet to a put (11)(12)(13)(14)(15)(16).

13

14

15

THE RECOVERY

As the shot leaves the hand, the force of the lift action results in the athlete leaving the surface of the circle. The right foot and leg are either left behind on the circle or picked straight up; both actions create the piked position of the hips on the release of the shot. This results in a very late reversal of the feet. Because of this right-leg action, there should be very little fouling (17).

16

The reversing of the feet is usually a natural result of the explosive release of the shot or of having to stay in the circle. The legs are well extended during the put, lifting the athlete off the surface of the circle. The reversal takes place at this time, with the right leg swinging to the stopboard and the left leg moving backward. On the landing of this turn jump, the impact of the body is absorbed by the slightly bent right leg (18).

17

Once the shot leaves the hand, the eyes must look downward to help lower the c.g. Fouls occur on many good throws because the athlete continues to "eyeball" the shot all the way out, keeping the c.g. too high. The most common fouling errors result from (19):
- uncontrolled speed across the circle
- the left side not blocking properly
- the hips sliding too far across the circle (sliding crotch).

18

19

John Godina, 1995 and 1997 Shot Put World Champion.

FAULTS AND CORRECTIONS

THE GLIDE

Fault: Shoulders and head turn to the left (open up) during the glide across the circle (20).

Correction: The athlete must concentrate on keeping the eyes focused on the rim to help control the head. A useful drill would be the use of a towel, one end of which the athlete holds in his left hand. The other end is held by the coach. The athlete glides across the circle as the coach holds the left shoulder back by pulling on the towel. When the athlete reaches the power position and is ready to throw, the coach lets go of the towel.

Another drill in which the coach can have "hands on" control of the athlete is to stand on the left side of the athlete with the coach's right hand placed gently on the athlete's left upper arm. As the athlete glides across the circle, the coach's hand keeps contact until the athlete reaches the power position. (The hand contact with the left arm, is merely a "reminder" for the athlete to keep the shoulders square, facing the rear of the circle.)

Fault: Late left foot to the front of the circle.

Correction: There are two possible problems. First, the left foot, even though the athlete extends it straight back, will initially lift above hip level. In this case, have the athlete sweep the left foot across the circle, keeping light contact with the surface as the foot reaches back for the board. The other possible problem is poor use of the left leg in terms of proper extension to the stopboard. The left foot must explode straight back to the stopboard and it must be trained to do so.

The A-Drill

Practice the A-Drill, in which the athlete, from the crouched position, drives the left foot back until only the right heel and left toes are in contact with the circle. Stop. Hold that position, making sure that the chest is on the right thigh, shoulders and head are square and facing to the rear, and the knees are "locked out" or straight (21).

Second drill: place a medicine ball directly behind the left foot and have the athlete punch or push the ball with the left foot as he drives the left foot back to the stopboard (22).

Rubber Cable Drills

Another drill that helps to eliminate this problem is the use of a rubber cable tied to the ankle of the left foot. The athlete can practice by holding onto a fence and punching the foot back repeatedly (23).

An added dimension would be to use the rubber cable attached to the left ankle while doing glides. The resistance forces the athlete to use the left leg more aggressively.

20

21

22

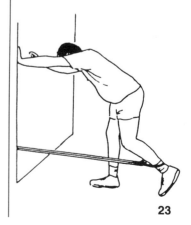

23

Fault: Hopping too high to the center of the circle.

Correction: This may be due to a lack of strength by the novice thrower. It is a common fault among young female athletes, so it is important that adequate leg strength be developed in the early stages of shot put training.

Another common cause of this fault is that the athlete drives up and off the ball of the right foot rather than rolling over the foot onto the heel as he drives to the front of the circle. Merely have him stand on a flat foot with the center of the gravity over the right heel. When he goes into the crouch position, keep the c.g. over the right heel. When he unseats, he will naturally roll off the right heel. Practicing the A-Drill can also help.

Fault: Right foot is too far under the body resulting in too narrow a base and the trunk extended too far back over the right leg (24).

Correction: The athlete throws the left foot so high to the rear during the glide that it causes the upper body to tilt forward. This reaction sometimes causes the athlete to pull the right foot out of the front of the circle too soon, resulting in the right foot traveling too far into the front half of the circle. The athlete must practice the A-Drill and similar drills to train the left-leg action. He should do a lot of imitations, concentrating on keeping the left leg locked at extension and having both feet plant at the *same* time, landing in a balanced power position.

Fault: Raising the trunk during the glide (25).

Correction: Lack of strength, again, may be the biggest reason. If the athlete possesses adequate strength, then it's just a poor habit. One indication of a lack of strength is that the athlete throws the left arm down and back, using it to help him glide across the circle. The athlete must realize that the legs do the work. He must concentrate on maintaining good "layback" or trunk lean to the rear, focusing his eyes on the rim (26).

Fault: During the glide, the head is down so that when the athlete lands in the power position, he looks as if he is looking under his armpit.

Correction: From this position, the athlete will invariably begin rotating before lifting with the back first, thus giving the appearance that he is looking through his armpit. He must line up correctly in the back of the circle, making sure that his head is in line with the trunk of the body. The coach lines the athlete's head up and tells him not to round the back or look down under the body. Keep the back fairly flat and the eyes on the rim of the circle.

Fault: The right foot during the glide deviates to the left side of the circle and the left foot is blocking the hips.

The O-Beam

Correction: Refer to the Training Chapter about the O-Beam. If an O-Beam is not available, the coach can use a 4x4 or even a 2x4 on which the athlete can practice the glide and even do the complete throw. Once the athlete is able to do the glide on the beam, he will be able to glide successfully in the circle.

24

INCORRECT — 25

CORRECT — 26

Fault: Begins rotating the shoulders to the left at the start of the glide, so that when the athlete lands in the center of the circle, the shoulders are facing the four or five o'clock position instead of the six o'clock position.

Correction: An athlete who has this fault will also usually rotate from the "bottom" (27) of the power position rather than lifting with the back and driving up over the left leg. The athlete must concentrate on keeping the shoulders square and keeping the shot in line with the right leg and foot. This is a matter of thinking and concentration on the part of the athlete.

Another method is to do imitations with a broom handle across the shoulders. The athlete does imitation glides using the broom handle to help him stay square with the back of the circle.

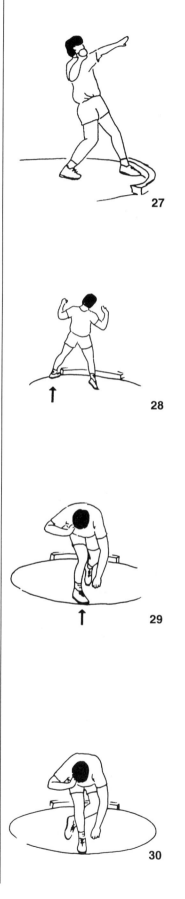

Fault: "In the bucket," a term frequently used to describe the placement of the left foot too far to the left or, in extreme cases, very near the left corner of the stopboard or even past it (28).

Correction: One of the causes is that, in the back of the circle, the athlete lines up so that the right foot is pointing to five o'clock (29). It is important that the athlete have his right foot direction at six o'clock.

Another cause is that while the thrower is in the crouched position, the left foot is brought up so that it is hooked behind the right knee (30). Then at the start of the glide, the left foot is pushed toward the ten or eleven o'clock position. Have the left foreleg parallel to the right foot which is pointing at six o'clock and in a line pointing straight back to the stopboard.

Many athletes prematurely turn the left foot out to the side resulting in the opening up of the hips, as well (31). There are two ways to correct these problems. One is to have the athlete concentrate on keeping the laces of the left shoe turned down toward the circle and not letting the foot turn out, so that the hips remain facing to the rear (32). At the last second, the hips turn out to assume the power position.

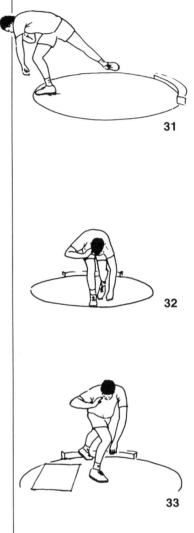

Another way is to place a towel in the left front half of the circle so that there is just enough room for the foot to land in the heel/toe alignment. This is merely a visual cue for the athlete to concentrate on and use his kinesthetic "feel" so he will not hit the towel with his foot (33).

Fault: Loss of balance at the back of the circle.

Correction: There are several reasons novice athletes experience loss of balance at the back of the circle. One is that they do not have the strength to support themselves in a single-support position when beginning to go into the crouch or when extending the left leg at the start of the glide. Novice athletes should not attempt to have the back parallel to the circle until they have sufficient strength to control the body. It is better to start them with a lay-back of only 45 degrees and then lower them as they develop better strength and balance.

Always have the novice athlete stand at the back of the circle with both feet in contact with the surface of the circle. Do not let him pick up the left foot and pull the left knee to the right knee until he is mentally ready and physically set and balanced. Do not allow him to stand there trying to balance on the right foot while he is adjusting himself to move the left knee forward.

Fault: The athlete is unable to pull the right leg to or near the center of the circle.

Correction: This is usually due to a lack of strength. Again, a good, solid weight training program is very necessary for an athlete to be able to perform with the proper technique.

A towel drill that can be used with good success is to place a hand towel on the circle directly behind the right heel. The athlete must pick the right foot up so that it does not touch this towel during the glide (34)(35).

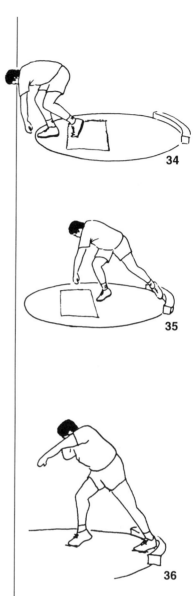

Another drill is to do imitations with the glide, not using the shot. Have athlete do the glide and land in the power position, attempting to have both feet land at the same time. Gradually, increase the distance until the athlete is going the prescribed distance. This drill works on two aspects of the glide: getting the right leg under the body and getting the left leg to plant soon after the right leg plants. (NOTE: Whenever we refer to "imitation" in this text, we mean practicing technique without the implement.)

Fault: The athlete settles back on the bent left leg so that the c.g. is over the left leg while the hips are still closed (36).

Correction: Have the athlete do a lot of glide imitations with a locked-out left leg, again emphasizing that both feet land at the same time. The athlete can do the same drill when practicing puts. The left leg is locked out so that the left side is blocked while the right side rotates around the left side.

Another point concerning technique would be to have the athlete start at the back of the circle with the trunk at a 45-degree angle, rather than have the back parallel to the circle. This will result in the athlete landing in a better balanced position, able to use the legs more efficiently.

THE PUT

Fault: The head is turned to the front during the left shoulder stretch of the chest, instead of keeping the eyes focused on the rim.

Correction: The athlete must concentrate on keeping the eyes "glued" to the rim. Another method is to keep the eyes on the right elbow until the shot is released.

Fault: The right shoulder and shot follow the left shoulder during the pre-stretch rather than keeping the shot on the straight path.

Correction: The athlete must concentrate on keeping the right shoulder back. The key is to keep the head back and have the shot follow a straight path from the back of the circle as if it were on an imaginary track.

Fault: Flat throw, with the athlete facing downward with the chest and head, rather than upward.

Correction: This is the result of poor right-leg push and turn and left-leg lift. It is remedied by having the athlete place his left foot on a four-inch box that is placed against the stopboard, with his right leg in the normal power position (37). The athlete must turn the right heel out as he pushes the right hip forward with the right leg, and he must finish on top of the box with both feet. It is important that the left leg lock out on the release of the shot.

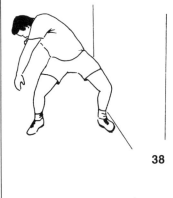

Left leg on 4" box or stopboard. 37

The Wall Drill

A useful drill to help left-leg lift is the Wall Drill. The athlete faces a wall so that his left foot/toes are up against the wall. Then the athlete torques and lowers the body into a standing put position with the left knee against the wall, as well. The athlete executes a standing put reaching up the wall with the right hand in a putting action. The extension of the left leg is as high as possible so that the athlete is up on the left toes and the right foot is lifted straight up and the toes are pointing down and backwards (38)(39).

38

39

Right Foot Wall Drill

This is another useful drill that develops left-leg lift, but emphasizes the lift upward and not forward, as the normal standing put could do. The athlete places the right foot flat against the wall so that only the toe touches the ground. The left foot is straight out in front of the right foot so that there is approximately a 90- to 100-degree angle in the left knee. This position will have the hips facing twelve o'clock. The shoulders and chest face three o'clock, placing the trunk in a torqued position.

With the shot at the athlete's neck, he bends the trunk to the right until the right elbow is against the wall. Be careful that the athlete does not lean forward or back while in this position. The back of the left hand is placed against the forehead.

It is critical when he puts the shot that the athlete drive up on the left foot until it leaves the ground explosively and it is even more critical that the right food slide up the wall, not losing contact.

Another cause of flat throwing is that the athlete does not have a good lifting action of the back which allows the right shoulder and shot to drive upward. He may also have poor right-leg extension to the front so that the right hip is not pushed to the front. All drills that train the right foot and leg to rotate to the front will also be effective.

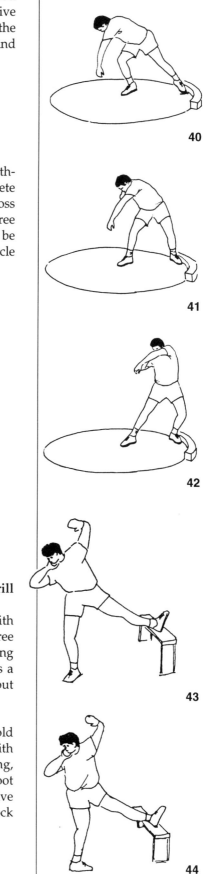

40

Fault: Sliding hip (sliding crotch). The athlete's hips move forward without turning to the front. If viewed from the back of the circle, the athlete appears to be falling backward as he puts the shot, literally putting across the chest. The hips and sometimes even the chest are facing at two or three o'clock at the time of the arm strike. The right leg and the foot must be trained to turn as soon as the right foot plants in the center of the circle (40)(41)(42).

41

42

The Impulse Drill

Corrections: The athlete places the inside of the left foot on a chair with the knee locked out straight. He turns the hips and shoulders to the three o'clock position, lowering the body by bending the right leg and turning the foot to the five o'clock position. He raises the right heel and does a series of right-foot rotations on the ball of the foot, turning the heel out until the toes and knee point to twelve o'clock (43)(44).

43

Another "impulse drill" would be a walking version. The athletes hold the shot in the normal position. He walks forward, taking a short step with the right foot turned out to the three o'clock position, followed by a long, reaching step with the left foot. As soon as the left foot lands, the right foot and leg rotate to the front, turning the heel out so that the toes face twelve o'clock. It is important that the shot and right shoulder face six o'clock throughout this drill.

44

31

The Step-Back Drill

This drill places emphasis on the right foot and leg rotating to the front and the blocking action of the left leg. This drill should be used after technique practice with an overweight implement to help develop specific strength.

The athlete stands with the outside of the left foot against the inside of the stopboard. The right foot is next to the left foot. He steps out with the right foot so that it lands slightly in the back half of the circle, pointing at four or five o'clock. The shoulders are torqued to the back so that they are facing six o'clock. The athlete is now in the power position.

It is imperative that the left leg stay locked out throughout the drill. The athlete lifts the right heel and then performs a standing put, lifting and snapping the shot out explosively (45)(46).

45

46

The Step-Back and Pull Drill

The drill starts out exactly as in the Step-Back drill, but this time the athlete steps even farther, a good foot-length farther than in the Step-Back drill.

The athlete pulls the foot back to the same position of the Step-Back Drill and performs a standing put as in the Step-Back drill. This is a very good specific strength drill when used with an overweight implement.

The Kneeling Drill

Correction: The athlete kneels down on the left knee (47). The right foot is six inches in front of the left knee with the c.g. directly over the right leg. The athlete's upper body is torqued to the right over the right leg and is laid back as if to perform a standing put.

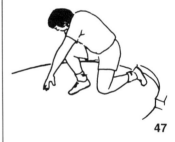

47

The athlete performs a standing put making sure that the right foot screws into the ground and the c.g. stays directly over the right leg during the put. Having to come up and put the shot forces the athlete to turn the foot, knee, and leg inward and to the front.

It is imperative that the head and shoulders remain to the rear with the eyes focused on the rim as long as possible. Also, the coach must watch for "Sliding Crotch." Some novices have a tendency to move the c.g. backward over the left leg as he stands up.

The same basic drill can be used with a 12-inch box (48). Instead of kneeling down, the athlete places his right foot on the box and assumes a standing put position. During the put, the c.g. *must* always stay over the right leg. This again forces the athlete to use the leg correctly.

In a variation of the above drill, the box is placed against the stopboard, and the athlete places his left foot on the box and assumes the standing put position. The athlete must finish the put on top of the box. This not only activates the turning of the right leg, but puts emphasis on the left-leg lift, as well (49)(50).

The Standing Put Towel Drill

The athlete assumes the power position. He holds one end of a towel and the coach holds the other end. The athlete performs a standing throw, never releasing his hold on the towel. As the athlete executes the throw, the towel passes over his head. This action forces the right leg and foot to turn and push the right hip to the front. Just as the athlete is about to put the shot, the coach lets go of the towel.

The same drill can be used as an imitation drill, only in this instance the coach does not let go of the towel, but forces the athlete to really push the hips to the front and rotate the right leg and foot. Rubber tubing can be used very effectively in place of the towel.

Another Rubber Cable Drill

A drill that helps to develop the right leg turn is done using a rubber cable. The athlete holds on to the end of the cable. (Some coaches have devised "handles" that look like shots that attach to the end of the rubber cable.)

The athlete assumes the standing put position. The cable is attached to the floor or the bottom of a fence or someone stands on the loose end. The athlete performs a standing put without an arm strike. He keeps his head back and rotates the right leg and knee in and the heel out, as the hip is pushed to the front. The stiff resistance of the rubber cable pulls the athlete off-balance if he does not perform the drill correctly (51)(52)(53).

51

52

Hands On Drill

53

Another drill used successfully is when the coach helps by turning the athlete's heel out and pushing his knee in. The athlete assumes the standing put position with the coach kneeling down on the athlete's open side. The coach's left hand cups the athlete's right heel and his right hand cups the athlete's right knee cap. As the athlete performs the standing put, the coach pulls the heel out and pushes the knee in.

Fault: Left side and shoulder drops and pulls away from the put, or the athlete allows the left arm to sweep down and away, pulling the left shoulder and chest away from the shot so that the shot goes down the left sector line. In most cases, the left leg is soft and bent, because the athlete does not lift at the time of release (54).

54

Correction: Practice left-leg drills that emphasize left-leg lift at the time of release. The left shoulder and arm block must be taught and practiced with a lot of imitation standing throws and with drills actually putting the shot. The athlete must be conscious of a high left elbow pulling the left shoulder to a high position that enables the right shoulder to follow and forcing the chest to drive upward. As the right arm strikes to release the shot the left arm is pulled back to the side of the body with the forearm parallel to the ground at shoulder height (55).

Fault: Instead of turning the right heel out during the put, the athlete rolls over the inner edge of the foot and heel, rather than pivoting on the ball of the foot and toes.

Correction: Use the preceding drills involved with turning the knee in and the heel out with emphasis on staying on the ball of the foot.

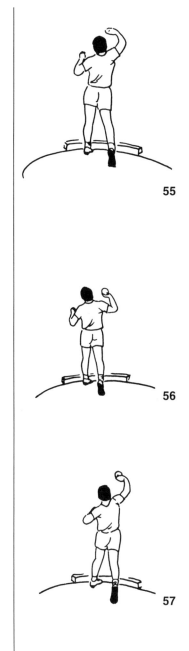

55

56

57

Fault: Dropping the elbow before putting the shot (56)(57).

Correction: Keeping the elbow up takes a great deal of concentration on the part of the athlete. If the problem persists, have the athlete slide the shot higher up the neck so that it is under the ear or even behind the ear. This forces the elbow up and results in the arm staying behind the shot during the put.

The Punch Drill

Another drill is the Punch Drill. The athlete stands with both feet/toes against the stopboard. He steps back with the right foot so that it is about three feet away from the board. He lowers his body by bending at the knees. He then leans back, arching the back. His left arm is pointing in the direction of the put. He punches the shot with the shoulder so that the deltoid or shoulder slaps against the right ear. He lifts the shoulder and "punches" the shot out, while, at the same time, he brings his left arm back in a "block" so that the arm is parallel to the ground.

Fault: During the arm strike, the arm rotates as if throwing a curve ball and the elbow is below the shot at release.

Correction: During the put, a conscious effort must be made to keep the elbow up and punch the shot out with a high elbow. The preceding drills may also be of some benefit.

THE SPIN TECHNIQUE

In major meets in the United States, the spin technique has become common and the glide is no longer completely dominant. In the European countries, on the other hand, the spin is a rarity.

In the 70s, two spinners had the farthest throws. In 1975, American Brian Oldfield threw an astounding 75'0", more than three feet farther than the world record. Though shot put cognoscenti accepted this mark as the world's best, it was not accepted by the IAAF as a world record since Oldfield was a professional. A year later, Aleksandr Barishnikov, a spinner from the USSR, threw 72' 2 1/4". This throw was accepted by the IAAF.

Gliders took over in 1978 and kept the world record for the next 12 years. Indeed, Italian putter Alessandro Andrei's 75'2" in 1987 surpassed Oldfield's mighty throw. This mark was later exceeded by East Germany's Ulf Timmermann in 1988 (75'8"). When head-on competitions took place between the top spinners and gliders, it seemed the glider was generally more consistent and stable under pressure.

But, during the summer of 1990, American Randy Barnes unleashed a series of throws to show the world that the spin was still alive, and there now seems to be no limit to what the spinner is capable of achieving. Barnes tossed the ball 75'10 1/4" and had practice throws over 76 feet . . . and one was reportedly 79 feet!

What makes the spin so explosive compared to the glide is the tremendous kinetic energy that can be generated from the back of the circle to the front and the powerful torque in the power position and the two-legged lift at the time of the release.

It can be inconsistent, yes. But when all the forces are in sync, the results can be dramatic. The athlete who uses the spin must learn to "live on the edge," be patient and endure hours of often-frustrating practice that is necessary for success. It's worth a try.

Experience shows that it is best to teach the novice the glide first, so that he will develop a good solid power position with a turning right leg. It is even more important that the turning inward of the right leg be developed for the spin.

Every thrower cannot be a spinner. The spinner must possess a certain temperament to be able to handle the precision of the technique. The athlete must be a totally dedicated person who cannot be wild or out of control. He must be a person who is not easily discouraged; he must possess tenacity. He has to be methodical and cool. The explosive urge must be under total control. One rule of thumb is that if a high school sophomore cannot reach 130-140 feet in the discus, he will probably not have the necessary rhythm or balance to become a successful shot put spinner.

THE STARTING POSITION

The shot is held in the hand exactly as in the glide. It can be held at the neck exactly as in the glide, but there is a trend by most spinners to hold the shot under or even behind the ear as Randy Barnes does. This is to help control the shot better during the turns.

The athlete straddles the midline of the circle with a base that is a little wider than his shoulders. This eventually adjusts according to individual preference and "comfort." The body is erect with shoulders square and facing the rear of the circle (60). The right hand holds the shot against the neck with the arm level with the shoulder and a 90-degree angle between

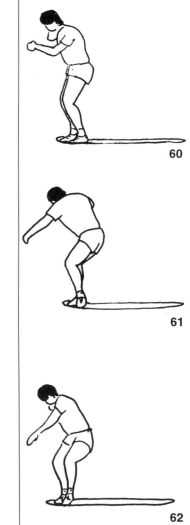

60

61

62

the arm and trunk. The left arm is at shoulder level and relaxed. It can be carried wide or slightly bent at the elbow in front of the body.

63

THE TURN

It is critical that the starting movements at the back of the circle are as perfect as possible as this will determine the success of the throw. After a slight rhythmical swing of the trunk to the right (61), the athlete begins a slow transfer of the c.g. to the left leg (62). The knees are bent 90 to 110 degrees, assuming a position similar to that of a front squat.

As the athlete pivots on the ball of the left foot, there is a delayed push-off of the right foot so that tension can be felt in the hip area, while, at the same time, the right arm and shot remain over the right knee and foot (63).

64

The left arm, which is slightly bent, is swept to the left until it is above the left knee and foot and continues to rotate with the knee and foot until they point to three o'clock (63). At this time, the right foot is picked up so that there is a 90-degree angle in the knee joint with the right knee leading the leg to the front. It is imperative that the angle be no less than 90 degrees. This shortening of the radius of the lower leg results in a quick tempo of the feet towards the center of the circle. This also assures a short and flat jump-turn (63)(64)(65)(66)(67).

65

66

67

The push-off comes from the foot and ankle only. The knee should never be locked out or straight as this will cause the athlete to jump too high and use up too much of the circle.

If the opening or swinging of the left arm is too vigorous, it will cause the upper body to fall into the turn resulting in a balance problem at the front of the circle.

One of the most basic points to be emphasized during the rotation out of the back of the circle is that the shoulders must stay level. Any dipping or dropping of a shoulder will result in a critical balance problem in the front of the circle (63)(64)(65).

As the body rotates to the front, off the left foot, the right foot is thrown to the center of the circle while the shoulders remain level, facing the direction of the throw (66)(67)(68).

The right toe and leg turn inward from the right hip so that when the right foot comes down, it is pointing to the nine o'clock position (69)(70).

Some athletes may find it helpful to focus the eyes to the front on some object to prevent an over-rotation of the shoulders as the left foot pushes the hips to the center of the circle. After the left foot has completed its push, it must be rapidly pulled close to the right leg and tucked under the hip for a successful throw.

The more effectively the left foot is pulled out of the back of the circle and is in a 90-degree relationship with the hips (70)(71)(72), the more efficient is the jump-turn to the power position, so that the left foot will not arrive late to the stopboard. Two coaching cues to help the athlete get the left foot to the front of the circle are to have him pull the left thigh as close to the right thigh as possible, or attempt to kick himself in the butt with his left heel.

68

69

70

71

72

It will be observed by the athlete, that when he picks the right lower leg up to the 90-degree angle at the back of the circle, the tempo of the feet quickens as a result of the shortened radius and throw of the right foot to the center of the circle. It is imperative that the right foot is picked up so that there is nearly a 90-degree angle in the knee. If there is a low or weak kick, the quick tempo reaction will not take place (65).

THE POWER POSITION

When the right foot makes contact with the circle, it is on the ball of the foot. The right heel must never come in contact with the circle throughout the rest of the throw, otherwise the foot cannot continue to rotate actively. The moment the heel comes down, the foot rotation is stopped. If the left leg and foot stay tucked under the left hip, the feet hit the ground with a quick tempo, resulting in much greater torque (shoulder-hip separation), and almost all of the weight is over a well-bent right leg (71)(72)(73).

73

When the left foot comes in contact with the surface, the shoulders must be square to the rear of the circle at the six o'clock position with the left arm wrapped across the chest. The hips face the three o'clock position and the feet are in a good left toe-right heel alignment. The base is narrower than the glide with the right foot anywhere from three to six inches in the front half of the circle (74)(75).

The left arm is wide and relaxed at about a 90-degree angle in relation to the front of the body, andthe right arm is still shoulder high, pressing the shot against the neck. This is the time when another focal point can be inserted to assure that the legs keep pivoting and the shoulders stay behind. When we speak of focal points, we are talking of a split-second eye contact on some object at the back of the circle (74).

74

The right foot remains on the ball of the foot and continues to turn aggressively to the front. At the same time, the legs must remain bent and not be allowed to straighten until the hips face the direction of the throw.

75

This is critical and very difficult to master. Nearly all spinners have to fight the problem where the left leg is straightened or locked out when the hips are still facing one or even two o'clock. This results in ineffective lift and release height and a put that slants toward the right sector line (76). The c.g. is predominately on the right leg and foot during the turning of the right hip in the direction of the put (75)(76).

THE PUT

The making of a great throw must come from both legs, but the critical primary source of lift comes from the left leg. This is necessary for an effective block of the left side, keeping the athlete in the circle and not fouling.

The timing must be "perfect." If the right leg lifts before the left leg, it often results in a throw down the left sector line and a weak block. There is also the danger of fouling. If the left leg lifts before the right leg, then the athlete is caught sitting or leaning back, with the c.g. behind the left leg, resulting in a weak and inefficient put.

The left arm has a critical function at the time of the actual put. As the right arm punches out to deliver the shot, the left arm is pulled down to the side of the chest. The timing of the left arm with the right is to facilitate the blocking of the left side, which will accelerate the right shoulder and arm action.

The head and chest are up, facing the direction of the throw as the right shoulder is punched up and the elbow is high behind the shot. The fingers and wrist execute a powerful "flick" with the thumb down and the little finger up as the shot leaves the hand (77)(78)(79)(80).

40

THE RECOVERY

The momentum developed by the action of the spin and leg lift results in the athlete spinning around and landing on a slightly flexed right leg, flat-footed and facing the nine o'clock position. The left leg is swung out wide toward six o'clock. The athlete may continue spinning one or two more times to gain control of the momentum (81)(82).

81

82

Randy Barnes set the world record in 1990—75-10¼ (23.12)—and won the 1996 Olympic title.

41

FAULTS AND CORRECTIONS

The coach will find that most of the errors that occur in the front of the circle are the result of errors committed in the back of the circle. It often takes a careful film analysis to discover these faults.

THE TURN

Fault: Over-rotation at the back of the circle during the rhythmical swing to the right can cause balance problems coming out of the back. This over-rotation can cause the athlete to fall into the circle when he begins to rotate back to the left over the left leg.

Correction: The athlete should be under control and not rush into the turn. He must concentrate on reducing the rhythmical swing to the right. In the shot, the upper body does not rotate as is done in the discus.

Fault: The head and left shoulder lead the body into the turn, causing the athlete to fall off-balance into the center of the circle.

Correction: The athlete should not rush into the turn. He should concentrate on shifting the weight to left, keeping the left arm and shoulder directly over the left leg. The head is in line with the trunk and the eyes are focused straight ahead, not looking to the left; the shoulders are level. As the left foot begins to rotate, he should keep the right foot down and not pick it up until the chest faces 3 o'clock.

Fault: Starting too fast out of the back of the circle and not allowing the weight or c.g. to stay on the left foot and leg during the turn.

Correction: The athlete must start slowly and be under control as he begins the turn to the left. If he starts too fast, he will have a tendency to fall back into the circle, have the shoulders lead the hips and be completely out of control and off-balance. Another problem that can occur if he comes out of the back of the circle too fast is that the excess momentum forces the c.g. over the left leg prematurely and results in the right foot being unable to rotate when in the center of the circle.

Fault: As the athlete reaches the three o'clock position with the hips, he drops the left shoulder. This causes the right shoulder and shot to fall ahead of the legs and the c.g. to fall to the left. The athlete loses his balance and literally falls out of the circle to the left after the put (83).

Correction: The shoulders must stay level. This merely takes concentration on the part of the athlete.

Fault: Weight falls back instead of shifting over the left leg. The athlete seems to fall seat-first into the circle even though the shoulders are level. This fault will always occur when the shoulders still face the six or five o'clock position.

Correction: The athlete must be sure that the c.g. passes onto the left leg and he is well-balanced. He should keep the left arm and shoulder over the left knee. With the weight over the left leg, he pivots to the left, keeping

83

the right foot in contact with the circle until the left foot and knee point to three o'clock.

Fault: The right knee and leg are lifted too high during the rotation out of the back of the circle when the right leg is pointing to five or six o'clock. This will cause the athlete to fall into the circle with the upper body toward the ten or eleven o'clock position. This affects his balance and results in him landing to the left of center and in the bucket.

Correction: This is often due to the athlete rushing out of the back of the circle too fast and picking the right foot up too soon so it is too high and out of control. He should slow down, keep the right thigh close to the left thigh. To help facilitate this, keep the right foot down until the shoulders face three o'clock.

Fault: As the athlete rotates on the left leg, he begins to straighten the left leg instead of keeping it well-bent at 90 to 110 degrees.

Correction: The athlete must concentrate on keeping the leg well-bent during the turn. A drill that emphasizes the bent left leg is practicing 360-degree turns on the left leg. The athlete stands facing the back of the circle. He then executes a 360-degree turn on the left foot until he is again facing the back of the circle. He should be able to do this under good control and with balance.

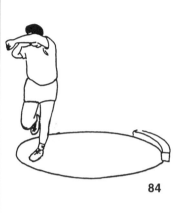

84

Fault: Rolling to the outer edge of the foot during the start of the first turn. This results in the athlete's c.g. passing outside of the left leg and the athlete having a tendency to fall into the turn because of poor balance (84).

Correction: The athlete should concentrate on staying on the ball of the foot (85) while doing hundreds of imitations of the turn in the back of the circle.

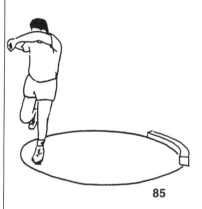

85

Fault: The athlete uses up too much of the circle coming out of the back of the circle. This often results in the athlete not having enough room for a good power position base.

Correction: This is often due to the athlete, once the left shoulder is facing the one or twelve o'clock position, dipping into the circle. Or the athlete rushes out of the back of the circle with the shoulders leading the hips and legs. He should keep the shoulders *level* and be sure that there is a 90-degree angle in the knee joint when the right foot is picked up. Also, it is imperative that he not pick up the right foot until the left foot and shoulders are facing three o'clock.

Fault: Over-rotation into the circle. This over-rotation can cause two faults at the time of release:
   (1) If the athlete over-rotates but is able to block with the left leg, he most likely will put the shot down the right sector line, even though the force vector of the body is to the left.
   (2) If there is not a left-leg block, the forces will be to the left and if the athlete does not foul, he will push the shot down the left sector line.

Correction: The athlete should keep the right foot on the circle until the shoulders and hips face three o'clock. Then when the right foot is thrown into the center of the circle, the athlete should pick a focal point at twelve o'clock and direct his drive toward it. Even though the athlete is spinning, this is still a linear event in which the athlete drives straight across the circle.

THE POWER POSITION

Fault: The left foot remains in the back of the circle when the right foot is about to settle in the center of the circle (86). The coach may find after a film analysis that the athlete has two other problems that may be attributed to the late left foot.

86

First, the late foot may be the cause of the left foot landing to the right of the right foot at the board (blocking the hips). This is a compound problem because the athlete has most likely stopped turning the right foot.

Second, he over-rotates. (He sort of pirouettes in the back of the circle.) The athlete backs into the front with his butt and the result is a left-foot landing in the bucket. The c.g. now passes from the right to the left leg before the complete turn of the hips to the front.

The Turn-and-a-Half Drill

Correction: Doing the Turn-and-a-Half Drill, the athlete stands at the back of the circle with the left foot inside the circle at the same spot that his foot would be if he were standing in preparation to do the full turn. He faces twelve o'clock and the right foot is outside of the circle. He pushes off from the right foot on to the left leg and then drives hard with the left leg to the center of the circle.

The athlete must concentrate on pulling the left foot as fast as he can behind the right knee and continuing into the power position and putting the shot. It is critical that the right foot is high on the ball of the foot and that it continues turning until it faces the direction of the throw. The left foot must come down as quickly as possible; in fact, the athlete should try to have both feet land at the same time.

Wheels

The Wheels Drill helps both the left foot tuck and the turning of the right foot. The athlete is in a power position with a broom handle across his shoulders, but with the hips closed or facing the same direction as the squared shoulders, right knee well-bent and the heel off the ground. The left foot is behind the right foot the basic power position distance, but the toes are facing the same direction as the right foot.

87

The athlete picks up the left foot and rapidly tucks it and spins on the right foot doing a 180-degree turn, maintaining the same position throughout the whole drill. This can be repeated several times in the same spot (87)(88). Coaching cue: Tell the athlete, "Kick yourself in the butt with the left heel." This will shorten the radius of the leg by bringing the foreleg up, resulting in a faster reaction.

Fault: The athlete is standing too upright when he gets to the center of the circle for the power position and does not have good lay-back.

Correction: The athlete must concentrate on his chest being down and his eyes focused on the rim of the circle at the six o'clock position. If the athlete

88

has good lay-back, the right elbow always points skyward as he plants the right foot in the center and is "waiting" for the left foot to ground next to the stopboard.

Fault: The right foot stops turning in the center when the heel drops. This, by far, is the most common and worst fault in the spin. The results is, in most cases, a "sliding crotch." When watched from behind, the athlete literally leans back and throws across the chest and invariably falls to the left out of the circle, if he is attacking hard (89)(90).

89

Correction: Hundreds and hundreds of imitation drills without the shot, working on that particular aspect of technique, making sure that the c.g. stays on top of the right foot and leg and not allowing the heel to touch the circle. Lots of Wheels and Turn-an- a-Half Drills are also helpful.

A modified Turn-and-a-Half Drill is to have the athlete stand facing the center, with the left foot in the circle at four o'clock and the right foot outside the circle. He throws the right foot to the center of the circle working the tuck of the left leg and pivoting on the right foot from this angle. This is quicker and assures that the right foot is landing in the eight or nine o'clock position.

90

Fault: Left leg straightens before the complete rotation of the hips to the front. When this happens, the hips and shoulders are facing one o'clock when the shot is released.

Correction: The legs must be kept well-bent throughout the whole rotation until the hips and shoulders face twelve o'clock. The athlete should keep the left leg "soft" until he is ready to drive up onto the left leg at the release of the shot. This is all timing and many imitations will help develop this aspect.

Fault: The base is too narrow, due to the right leg "eating up" too much of the circle (91).

91

Correction: The athlete must work on the "impulse" aspect of the turn from the back of the circle. He must not pick the right foot up too quickly, but wait until the hips, left foot and shoulders are facing the three o'clock position. It is imperative that there be a 90-degree angle in the right knee when the right foot is picked up.

The athlete may also be falling into the center of the circle because he has lost his balance due to poor technique in the turn. Refer to corrections that are prescribed under The Turn of the Faults and Correction section.

Valentina Fedyushina of Russia threw 67-7 (20.60) in 1992.

TEACHING PROGRESSION FOR THE SHOT PUT GLIDE

The throwing events use the part-whole-part method of teaching. The coach breaks the event down into parts. In the case of the shot put, the power position is taught first, then the glide. After the athlete seems to have acquired a certain amount of skill for these parts, the two are combined into the whole so that the athlete learns the rhythm of the event.

The coach must use most of the technique time on the "whole" event for timing and rhythm, but the athlete is required to practice parts of the event to reinforce certain aspects that may be causing him trouble, using the drills described previously to make these corrections.

The novice athlete must be convinced that the legs are the most important part of the body in throwing the shot. To accomplish this, the athlete is asked to do certain throws that demonstrate how each part of the body affects the distance of the throw, if the sequential timing is in place. Each step eventually leads into the complete throw.

Step One: Teach the athlete how to hold the shot properly on the neck.

Step Two: Teach the athlete how the shot must be released from the hand and how the arm must be positioned during the arm strike. Have the athlete hold the shot in both hands so the thumbs are down and the little fingers are up. The shot is held at the chest as if it is for a basketball chest pass. The elbows are up so that they are parallel to the ground. The athlete pushes the shot out so that there is a wrist flick with the thumbs down and the little fingers up.

Step Three: Use the same drill as step two, except that the shot is moved to the neck and shoulder. The athlete steps forward with the left foot, turns the trunk to the right and puts the shot. The shot is put primarily with the right hand, being sure that the thumb is down and the little finger is up.

Step Four: The purpose of the next three steps is to demonstrate the importance of the legs and oblique muscles. The athlete stands with both feet against the stopboard. The shot is placed at the neck as taught in Step One. Without bending the legs, or turning the trunk to the right, the athlete puts the shot using the arm only. The coach marks the distance with a cone or some other object.

Step Five: The athlete is in the same position assumed in Step Four, only this time without bending the legs, he rotates the trunk to the right and puts the shot. The coach marks the distance, which should be much farther than the first throw with the arm only.

Step Six: The athlete keeps the left foot against the board, but this time steps back with the right foot, bends the knees, rotates to the right and puts the shot. The coach again marks the distance and points out that there is a difference in distances when the body parts are used in proper sequence and that the legs contribute 70% to the distance in shot putting.

Step Seven: Teaching the power position. Have the athlete place a broom handle held in his hands on his chest in the clean position. He spreads his feet a good foot or so wider than his shoulders in a right heel-left toe alignment. The left foot is pointing to the three o'clock position and the right is pointing to five o'clock.

He squats down, bending the knees, and turns the trunk of the body to the right. He bends at the waist over the right leg. The weight should shift to the right leg so that the left leg is straight or even locked out at the knee. The hips face three o'clock and the shoulders and head are facing six o'clock. Raise the right heel.

The position should be such that a straight line could be drawn through the left shoulder, left hip and foot. The athlete should feel the torque or tension in the waist. The coach will adjust the trunk angle, head position, left leg position, etc., until the athlete is in a "perfect position." The athlete must kinesthetically feel where every body part must be.

Step Eight: The athlete assumes the same position as in Step Seven still using the broom handle. The first movement is a lifting of the back and pushing with the right leg and the ball of foot until the c.g. is over the left leg and the shoulders and trunk face twelve o'clock. The rotation of the shoulders to the front will be a natural reaction if the legs are used properly. *It is important that the eyes are focused on the rim at the back of the circle during the whole lifting action.* If the legs are used properly, the right foot and knee will be facing twelve o'clock.

Step Nine: Without a shot in the hand, the athlete does imitation throws, emphasizing the explosive push of the right leg which pushes the hip to the front. The athlete must also be taught the left arm action and the left side block. Go through each function step by step slowly so that the athlete understands the action. The following points of technique must be critically schooled:

    a.   Right heel turns out and the right knee turns in.

    b.   Head and eyes must stay focused on the rim at the back of the circle.

    c.   When the left arm/elbow point in the direction of the throw, the chest is brought to the left arm, blocking the left side.

    d.   The athlete must drive on top of the left leg and toes at the time of the arm strike.

    e.   The right arm strike is a high punching action so that the right shoulder is above the left shoulder and the right elbow and arm are behind the shot.

    f.   The athlete *must lift first,* trying to keep the shot in a straight path to the front, as if it were on a track.

        The Power Position is not a static position, so we believe that after the athlete understands and "feels" the position of a "static" power position, it is time to introduce a "dynamic" standing put.

        The athlete stands in the center of the circle with the right foot six inches in the back half of the circle and the feet together. He bends his knees 100-110 degrees and turns the trunk to the right until the shoulders are facing six o'clock. He leans forward in the lay-back position and reaches dynamically with the left foot for the stopboard. As soon as his left foot slams against the stopboard, the right leg drives forward with the heel turning out, and he executes a standing throw.

        When the coach is satisfied that the athlete is able to demonstrate a certain amount of skill with the imitation throw, he then has him use a light implement. It must be light enough so that it does not alter the technique too much.

        There are many drills in the Faults and Corrections sections that can be used to help the athlete acquire the standing throw and overcome complex intricacies that can plague him. See the problem, determine the cause, and then use the correcting drill.

        This particular step may take days and even weeks, depending upon the athlete. The coach must not advance to the glide until the athlete can do a standing throw with a certain amount of skill.

Step Ten: Drills are needed to help the athlete develop the kinesthetic feel of the left leg drive, the unseating of the hips and the push with the right leg.

    a.   The athlete bends over until his back is parallel to the ground using a fence as support. He sinks down on the right leg with the knees together, drives the left leg back and down, locking out the knee. He repeats this action several times.

    b.   Drills that can help the athlete develop a feel for the left-leg action involve the use of the medicine ball and rubber cable (refer to Fault and Corrections section).

Step Eleven: The glide across the circle.

    a.   Do the A-Drill (refer to the Fault and Correction section.) Once the athlete understands the unseating, left-leg extension, right-leg push, and the right heel off the circle *last,* he goes to the next step.

b. Have the athlete attempt a glide to the power position. How well the left foot is extended toward the stopboard, how good his lay-back is, how square his shoulders are, how his head is positioned—these are the important points. The distance of the glide comes naturally with the acquisition of strength and skill. Do not force the athlete to attempt a glide any longer than he can handle and still land in a well-balanced power position.

c. If there is difficulty, drills such as the Towel Drill can be used.

Step Twelve: Now is the time to put it all together. Have the athlete glide to the power position and stop. Check and correct his power position. During the first attempts to put it all together, balance becomes a real problem and the athlete might have to stop to correct his power position and then proceed to put the shot. The stops become small delays until there is no stopping. Now it becomes rhythm, timing and many hours of practice.

Astrid Kumbernuss of Germany, top woman shot putter of the 90's.

TEACHING PROGRESSION FOR THE SHOT PUT SPIN

Step One: Teach the glide first. After the athlete has "mastered" the glide, the coach must determine if he has the right temperament, athletic ability, and balance to handle the spin. A good indicator would be the ability to throw the discus 130-140 feet.

Step Two: Have the athlete do the Wheel Drill with the shot. After he is able to do the 180-degree turns with good balance, keeping the heel up and never shutting the turning foot down, introduce the standing spin put.

    a. The athlete has his right foot in the center of the circle, heel up and facing ten o'clock. He spins on the right foot, picks up the left while trying to maintain a 90-degree angle between the foot and the hips, and plants the left foot and puts the shot.

    b. When the left foot touches the circle he must push the right hip to the front and drive up with both legs.

Step Three: The athlete faces the same direction as he does in Step Two, only this time the left foot is inside the circle on the four o'clock position and the right foot is outside. He takes a jump-turn to the center of the circle and does an active pivot on the right foot and puts the shot.

Step Four: The Three-Quarter Drill. The athlete sets up in the back of the circle as he would at the start for the complete throw. Once he has established a good basic athletic position, he pivots on the balls of his feet until he is facing three o'clock. The athlete puts his hand to the neck as if he is holding a shot, the left arm is held out in front, relaxed, at shoulder level and curved in to the center.

While in this position, he shifts his weight onto the left leg and pivots to the left. When the left foot faces twelve o'clock, the right foot is picked up so that there is a 90-degree angle in the knee and it is kicked or thrown to the center of the circle. When the right foot lands in the center of the circle, the left foot remains at the back of the circle. While the athlete holds this position, the coach checks to see that his shoulders are level and the chest is facing twelve o'clock and right shoulder is held behind the right hip.

Step Five: Same drill as Step Four, except when the right foot is thrown to the center of the circle, the left foot is pulled out of the back of the circle as quickly as possible and the athlete pivots on the right foot keeping the weight directly over the right leg. He lands in a good power position and does an imitation put. (Coaching cue: To keep the shoulders level and prevent backing into the circle tell the athlete to pick a focal point in the twelve o'clock direction and drive straight at it when he throws the right foot to the center of the circle.)

Step Six: After the athlete can do Step Five with good technique, then have the athlete use a shot. An underweight implement is preferable at this time. The most important points the coach must watch for are:

    a. the weight over to the left leg at the start of the turn

    b. keep the left arm directly over the left leg; do not allow the left shoulder to pull ahead of the left leg

    c. right leg pickup and a 90-degree angle in the knee at the back of the circle

    d. the right foot thrown to the center of the circle

    e. the shoulders level as he drives to the center of the circle

    f. no delay in getting the left foot to the front of the circle

    g. the weight staying directly over the right leg when in the center of the circle

    h. the right heel never touching the ground

    i. the lift/block of the left leg during the release of the shot.

Step Seven: The full turn. The athlete begins by doing a series of imitations. Then when the coach believes that he has the "feel," the athlete uses an implement. It is critical, at the back of the circle, that the athlete not pick up the right foot until the shoulders/hips face three o'clock. As the athlete practices, the coach deals with problems as described in the Faults and Corrections section for the Spin.

The spin, as practiced by former American record holder Dave Laut.

DISCUS THROW

Al Oerter

DISCUS THROW

STARTING POSITION AND GRIP

The athlete stands in the back of the circle facing the six o'clock position, straddling the line that would divide the circle in half. The feet are about shoulder width apart with the weight between the legs. The discus is held in the fingers of the right hand, primarily the middle and forefinger. The tips of the fingers are curled around the edge of the discus at the first joint. (There are two ways the athlete can spread the fingers: one is where the fingers are spread about a half-inch apart and the other is when the forefinger and middle finger are pressed together.) The wrist is slightly bent so the upper edge of the discus rests against the inner arm and the hollow of the hand never touches the discus.

THE WINDUP

Even though there are many different ways in which the athlete may start his windup, the most common one which enables the athlete to begin with a stable hand position is where the discus is held high in front of the left shoulder, resting on the left palm with the right hand on top of the discus. The discus is swung back to the right at shoulder level with the back of the hand facing upward where it is "caught" behind the back.

There should be not more than one or two preliminary swings before the start of the turn. The preliminary swing is to help the athlete relax and set up a rhythm to start the turn and to get the discus behind the body for a long acceleration path.

THE TURN

When the discus is swung back behind the right side of the body, the weight is transferred to the right leg (1). It is important to keep the radius of the discus as wide as possible, so it is necessary to keep the discus at shoulder level. The greater the radius, the greater the angular velocity and linear speed of the discus.

The left arm is shoulder high and, as the discus is swung behind the body, the arm is slightly wrapped across the front of the chest. The body is erect and the head and eyes are focused on the horizon.

When the discus reaches the maximum point behind the body, the weight is shifted to the left leg (2), as the body is lowered to a "sitting position" with a 100- to 110-degree bend in the knees.

There is a slight bend in the trunk as the legs begin pivoting to the left on the balls of the feet. The c.g. is shifted directly over the ball of the left foot. When the left foot is pointing to about three o'clock (3), only then does the right foot push off from the back of the circle.

As the body continues to pivot on the left foot, the right shoulder and trailing arm and discus are behind the right hip, producing torque between the trunk and the lower part of the body. The left arm is wide with the left armpit directly over the left knee; the head and eyes are still focused on the horizon.

The shoulders are level, as balance is very critical throughout the turn as head and eyes are focused on the horizon.

1

2

3

When the hips and shoulders are facing three o'clock and the toes of the left foot are pointing to one or two, only then is the right foot picked up.

When the right leg is at about four to five o'clock (4), the body is in a Reverse-C position in which the left hip is pushed out to the center of the circle. This is illustrated well by all throwers who have good balance and demonstrate good drag of the right arm and discus behind the right hip.

The novice thrower very often is seen with the trunk ahead of the hips or the left shoulder "falling" into the center of the circle, off-balance. The athlete must stay on a well-bent left leg while the right leg leads the body around.

As the right leg is picked up, it is imperative that there is a good 90-degree angle in the knee joint. As soon as the right foot is picked up, it is thrown or kicked to the center of the circle. The foot lands on the ball of the foot as quickly and dynamically as possible with the heel never touching the circle.

While the body is in flight during the jump-turn (5), the left leg must be quickly tucked under the left hip and next to the right thigh creating a 90-degree relationship between the foot and the hips. The left arm is brought in closer to the body. This helps to facilitate an increase of angular momentum (6).

The drive off the left foot is from the ankle joint without straightening the knee, thus enabling the left foot to get to the front of the circle as quickly as possible. A common error made by many athletes takes place at the time they are putting the right foot down in the center of the circle. Just as the right foot is making contact, the athlete is pulling the left foot late out of the back of the circle.

There must be a quick withdrawal of the left foot from the back of the circle for the quick tempo of the feet in the front half of the circle. This is necessary for a long pull on the discus. The longer it takes to put the left foot down, the shorter the pull on the discus.

It is very important that when the right foot hits the center of the circle, there is no lowering or raising of the body from the right leg. Any deviation in the angle of the right knee will have an effect upon the fluid transition from the power position to the release of the discus.

THE POWER POSITION

The most important aspect of the power position is landing in a strong, balanced position. If the athlete does not land in a good, balanced stance, he will not be able to get maximum pull on the discus. Balance is predetermined by what the athlete does in the back half of the circle.

The right foot should land about three inches in the front half of the circle, with the toes pointing from nine to six o'clock, on the ball of the foot with the shoulders square to the six o'clock position and directly over the right foot. A coaching cue at this point is to have the athlete drive straight toward a predetermined focal point so that he does not "back into" the circle by overturning out of the back of the circle. The heels should never touch the circle during the rest of the throw.

The left arm is wide across the chest; the trunk is bent forward with a 90- to 100-degree bend between the trunk and the right thigh. The left foot lands 24 to 32 inches behind the right foot in a right heel-left toe alignment.

An error many novice throwers make at this point is to reach forward toward the front of the rim with the left foot so that the c.g. slides to the left leg instead of staying on top of the right leg. If the athlete is in a correct power position, a straight line can be drawn from the left shoulder, down through the left hip and left ankle the moment the left foot touches (7).

If the athlete lands in a well-balanced power position, the discus is naturally going to be high (7) for the downward sweep. The right leg stays well-bent as the discus begins its downward path toward the back of the circle due to the aggressive turning of the right foot and leg.

When the left foot touches the circle, the discus should be anywhere from the nine to eleven o'clock position. This allows for at least a 270-degree arc (7) for the discus to be pulled through before the release.

THE DELIVERY

When the right foot lands, it must *never* stop rotating as it pulls the right side around the braced left side of the body which is acting like a hinge. It is most important that the weight stay on the right leg and foot during this whole phase.

When the discus has reached the six o'clock position (8), which is the lowest point in the path of the discus, the hips must be thrust forward aggressively by the turning right leg. This drives the hips and chest "against" the braced left leg and shoulder, producing a "snapping action" that allows the right arm and shoulder to whip the discus out of the hand.

It is critical that the left shoulder *not* move back during this phase as the hips are blasted forward against the braced left leg, thus producing an arching of the long axis when the hips press forward.

The right leg should be locked out as it pushes the right hip forward so that the weight is approximately 60% on the locked-out left leg and 40% on the right leg (9).

When the discus leaves the hand, it comes off the forefinger in a clockwise rotation, shoulder high, with the back of the hand up. The outside edge of the discus is down, while the leading edge is up about eight to ten degrees. The discus leaves the hand at 90 degrees to the side or the three o'clock position (10).

The position of the hand and the level of the arm have great influence on the different angles at the time of release. These angles——the angle of release and angle of incidence of the discus while in the air——are just as important as the height of release and the speed of release. Therefore, it is imperative that consideration be given to the hand position at the time of release.

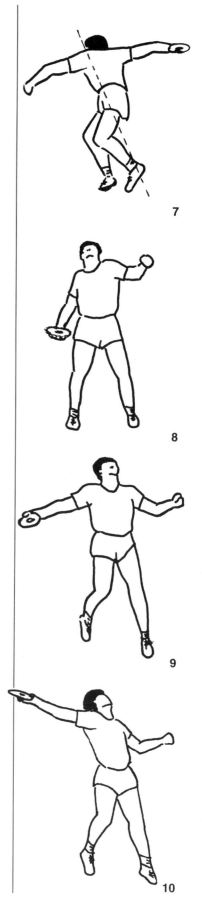

7

8

9

10

THE RECOVERY

After the release of the discus (11), the athlete must reverse the feet to stay in the circle. The right foot is brought forward to the front of the circle and absorbs the body's impact by landing on a softly bent knee, while the left leg is swung back to the six o'clock position and the trunk and shoulders face nine o'clock.

If the athlete has a good block, it is easy to watch the flight of the discus. Some elite athletes hold the block so well that they do not reverse until well after the discus has left the hand.

11

World record holder Jürgen Schult releases the discus.

FAULTS AND CORRECTIONS

STARTING POSITION

Fault: Preliminary swing too high as the athlete bends too far forward during the back swing (12).

12

Correction: Keep the body upright, with only a slight bend in the trunk (13).

13

Fault: Discus is too low, below shoulder level.

Correction: The athlete must concentrate on swinging the discus at shoulder level.

THE WINDUP AND TURN

Fault: During the swing back to the right, the novice rotates the hand and discus so that when the discus catches in the back, the discus is facing up, with the back of the hand facing down.

Correction: The athlete lacks confidence in the centrifugal force holding the discus in the hand. Have the athlete stand as if in the back of the circle. He starts with the discus sitting on the upturned left hand in front of the left shoulder (14). Then he takes the discus in the right hand and does a series of swings with the back of the hand up to realize that the discus will stay in the hand as it keeps moving.

14

Another drill is to do a series of 360-degree turns with the discus held out at shoulder height so that the novice knows that the discus will stay in the hand.

Doing the Three-Quarter Drill helps develop more confidence with the discus in the hand before the athlete goes to the full turn. The drill is done by having the athlete start out by facing the three o'clock position with the left foot in the circle and the right foot outside the back of the circle. He must concentrate on keeping the back of the hand up as he progresses through the drill and releases the discus.

Fault: The athlete pivots on the left heel out of the back of the circle. The athlete may be falling backward as he starts the turn, instead of transferring his weight directly over the left leg and foot.

Correction: Have him slow down and shift his weight to the ball of the left foot with a slight body lean. He must concentrate on pivoting on the ball of the left foot.

Fault: Left arm and shoulder lead the hips and leg into the center of the circle because the athlete starts the turn with the upper body (15).

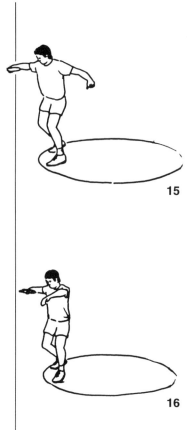

15

Correction: In almost all cases the athlete begins the turn with a aggressive sweep of the left arm, pulling the upper body with it, leading the lower body. The athlete should start slowly and concentrate on keeping the left shoulder and arm above the pivoting left leg and foot (16).

16

Fault: When the right leg is picked up, the athlete lifts the right leg too high toward six o'clock, thus causing the body to tilt in toward the center of the circle and the athlete to fall off-balance into the circle.

Correction: The athlete must start slowly, keep the shoulders level and not pick the foot up too aggressively. He should keep the eyes on the horizon and the left shoulder over the left leg and foot.

Fault: The athlete over-rotates in the back of the circle. Rather than driving to the center of the circle, the athlete is literally "pirouetting" in the back of the circle.

Correction: The athlete should pick a focal point and drive his right shoulder and chest toward the front of the circle in a linear path.

Fault: Weight falls backward into the circle, usually because the thrower does not transfer the c.g. completely over the left leg.

Correction: The athlete should go slowly, lean his body slightly forward and do many practice turns concentrating on transferring his weight to the left leg and pivoting on the ball of the foot. There's no substitute for repetition, repetition and more repetition to make the proper movements "second nature."

Fault: The athlete dips the left shoulder into the center of the circle during the rotation out of the back of the circle while the chest is facing three o'clock. This will affect his balance and will create premature shifting of the c.g. over the left leg instead of it remaining on top of the right leg during the power position.

Correction: The use of a long piece of PVC across the shoulders of the athlete as he does repeated turns out of the back of the circle and imitates the complete discus throw. The PVC will help the athlete to develop a kinesthetic feel of level shoulders during the turn out of the back of the circle.

Fault: Jump-turn too short.

Correction: The athlete is not driving off the left foot and not throwing the right foot to the center of the circle. He should do practice turns using marks as targets. The marks are graduated lines that the athlete attempts to reach, trying to go farther each turn, driving off the left foot and kicking or throwing the right foot to the center of the circle.

Fault: Turn decelerates, because the athlete jumps too high out of the back of the circle. When the athlete is in the air, there is no application of force; thus the longer the athlete is not in contact with the circle, the greater the loss of acceleration.

Correction: The athlete is jumping straight up, using the left leg incorrectly. The jump-turn must be initiated from the foot and ankle so that the left knee is *not* locked out. The push should come from the ankle. The athlete should not use the left leg so vigorously that the left knee straightens out. Also, if there is a vigorous throw or kick of the right foot to the center of the circle, this action will result in a low jump-turn.

Fault: The athlete raises up on left leg as he pivots to the left. This is a common fault with novice throwers.

Correction: The athlete must concentrate on staying down on the left leg and keeping the knees well-bent. This requires a lot of imitations. Doing 360-degree turns on the left leg will help the athlete develop the ability to maintain the proper knee bend throughout the turn.

17

THE POWER POSITION

Fault: Late left foot.

Correction: The athlete must learn to pull the left leg under the hip and close to the right thigh as soon as possible before the right foot lands in the center of the circle. There are different drills the athlete can do to train this foot action. First, there is the Wheel Drill. The athlete gets into the power position and pivots quickly doing 180-degree turns, getting the left foot down as quickly as possible. He should keep the weight well over the bent right leg and maintain a 90-degree relation between the hips and the left foot (17)(18).

18

A cue for the coach to use is to tell the athlete to try to kick himself in the butt with his left foot. This will shorten the radius of the left leg to speed the action to the front.

When it is time to pick the right foot up during the turn at the back of the circle (being sure that there is a 90-degree angle in the knee), the throwing of the right foot to the center of the circle results in an impulse action that causes a very quick tempo of the feet to the front of the circle. There should be a lot of imitation practices of this particular aspect of the technique.

In extreme cases of the left foot being very late, especially among novices, the coach can see, when analyzing film, that the left leg is still in front of the body after the right foot has set down in the center and the shoulders are facing six o'clock. Again, a lot of work on Wheels and some of the other drills noted above is necessary.

Fault: Left arm and shoulder open up.

Correction: This may be due to the right foot "shutting down." The right foot must continue to pivot aggressively. If the heel drops so that the foot cannot rotate, the shoulders continue to rotate while the hips stay closed and the c.g. continues to move forward to the left leg. The fault may also be the result of a very late left foot so that when it finally comes down, the left shoulder is pointing to twelve o'clock (19).

The athlete should do Wheels while concentrating on keeping the weight over the right leg. Again, the left arm should be pointing to the six o'clock position when the left foot touches down.

19

Fault: Reaching with the left foot. Many new throwers reach or push the left foot way to the front when trying to "muscle" or "kill" the discus. They shut the right foot down and literally reach far forward with the left foot so that the base is very wide and the c.g. is between the legs and the throw is done with the upper body.

Correction: The athlete must concentrate on keeping the weight over the right leg, with the right heel up and the legs doing the work. He must relax and not attempt to muscle the discus. He should do a lot of Wheels and imitations.

Fault: Left foot "in the bucket."

Correction: This could be the result of a couple of problems: over-rotation out of the back of the circle or the loss of balance out of the back of the circle. To overcome the over-rotation, have the athlete use a focal point and drive the right shoulder toward it. The loss of balance is most likely due to the dropping of the left shoulder into the center of the circle or coming out of the back too fast and out of control. Another common cause is the shutting down of the right foot, which results in the athlete having to reach to the left with his left foot so that he can deliver the discus.

Fault: Center of gravity/weight is not on top of the right leg, because the right foot shuts down and stops pivoting (20), causing the hips to slide to the front so that the c.g is on top of the left leg.

Correction: When the right foot stops rotating and the right heel drops, the left foot lands late. This results in the hips sliding back over the left leg.

20

The athlete should do Wheels, right-foot drills, the Turn-and-a-Half Drill, and the Three-Quarter Drill, with emphasis on staying on top of that right leg and screwing the foot into the circle.

The Modified Turn-and-a-Half Drill

The athlete has the left foot inside the circle at the four o'clock position. He drives off the left foot, throwing the right foot to the center of the circle, and he works the right foot aggressively with the weight over the right leg.

Fault: Discus is too low or below the shoulder when the left foot lands at the front of the circle, usually because the athlete is not in a good lay-back position. He is standing up too high or straight which leads to other complications, such as the c.g. over the left leg.

Correction: The athlete should do Standing-Throw Pivots, making sure that he is in a good lay-back position. If the discus is carried at shoulder level, then the discus will always be at the proper height (21)(22). From here, the athlete can practice some of the previous drills, such as the 180-Degree Drill in which he throws the arm and discus into the air in the direction he is going to throw and runs under the discus to get into a good lay-back position.

Sink-and-Sling Drill

Another drill is the Sink-and-Sling Drill. The athlete stands with the weight on the right foot and the left foot back 24 to 32 inches. He then sinks down on the right leg. At the same time, he throws the discus back as he goes into a good lay-back position from where he completes the delivery. The athlete should not settle or slide backwards onto the left leg as he sinks on the right (23)(24)(25).

21

22

23

24

25

THE DELIVERY

Fault: Center of gravity/weight slides back onto the left leg (26).

Correction: The right foot has stopped rotating and as the athlete continues through the delivery, the c.g. moves onto the left leg. It also may be due to a soft left leg that allows the c.g. to move over the left leg as the right side is pushed forward. The left leg must stay firm and resist the rotating right side.

    The athlete should do standing throws, the 180-Degree Drill, etc., where he concentrates on the rotation of the right foot and a firm left leg. Do the Sink-and-Sling Drill, concentrating on a firm left leg during the pivot and locking out the left leg at release. And do Sink-and-Sling drills so that at the release, the left leg is lifted off the ground forcing the athlete to pivot and stay on the right leg.

Fault: The thrower does not straighten the right leg on final thrust at time of the release and is sitting back over the right leg instead of up over the locked-out left leg (27).

Correction: The athlete should do a lot of standing throws where he drives up so that both legs will straighten out. Do not allow the athlete to reverse his feet. Then he should go to more complicated drills such as the Turn-and-a-Half Drill and the Sink-and-Sling. Always emphasize the complete extension of both legs.

Fault: Left arm and shoulder do not stop to block, but continue to move backward.

Correction: The athlete should do standing throws, striving to stop the left shoulder and arm at the same time as the right and left legs straighten out and the discus release takes place.

Fault: Poor left leg block. Left leg is allowed to stay soft, and at the time of release, the left knee is still bent (28).

Correction: The athlete should do standing throws, Sink-and-Sling, and the Turn-and-a-Half Drill, always stressing that the left leg locks out at the time of release.

Fault: Full extension of the legs does not take place at the time of the release.

Correction: Straighten both legs at the same time when doing standing throws (29).

Fault: Dropping the discus below shoulder level.

Correction: The athlete should do standing throws concentrating on keeping the discus at shoulder level and the arm extended as far as possible.

Fault: Palm faces the direction of the throw (this opens the hand up), so that the thumb is facing upward.

Correction: The athlete must press the thumb down, yet still keep the outside edge of the discus slightly down.

Fault: Right leg loses ground contact too soon, so that weight goes to the left leg too soon.

Correction: The athlete should do all throws without reversing the feet.

Fault: Feet reverse before release of the discus.

Correction: The athlete should do all throws without reversing the feet.

Fault: Feet reverse at time of the release.

Correction: The athlete should do all throws without reversing the feet.

Fault: Discus comes out of the back of the hand.

The Bowling Drill

Correction: The athlete should roll the discus on the ground or toss it in the air using a bowling-type action, closing the thumb and forefinger in a pinching action.

Fault: The left shoulder drops drastically, and the left leg bends at the time of release. This is the result of the athlete compensating for the shutting down of the right foot. He literally pulls the left shoulder hard to the left to be able to release the discus. He pulls the discus across his chest with the hips still facing the three o'clock position.

Correction: The athlete should do all previous drills that emphasize training in the rotation of the right foot and leg.

The No. 1 discus man of the 90's, Lars Riedel of Germany.

TEACHING PROGRESSION FOR THE DISCUS

The novice athlete must understand that the legs are the key to success in the discus. If he understands this, he will understand the nature of many of the drills and the teaching progressions that are used.

Step One: Teach the athlete how to hold the discus. Refer to the discus section on the two different methods of holding the discus.

Step Two: Teach the release of the discus from the hand. There are two drills that help the athlete learn how the discus leaves the hand in a counter-clockwise motion off the forefinger.

    a.   Bowling the discus. The discus is released from the hand using the same arm action as in bowling. When the discus leaves the hand, the athlete closes the thumb and forefinger in a pinching manner.

    b.   Tossing the discus in the air. The athlete swings the arm so that the discus is tossed into the air, using the pinching action so that the discus comes off the forefinger.

Step Three: Develop confidence in the athlete so he realizes that the discus will stay in his hand as long as his arm is kept in motion.

    a.   The discus is placed in the upturned palm of the left hand which is in front of the left shoulder.

    b.   The right hand is placed on top of the discus and properly gripped.

    c.   The athlete proceeds to swing the discus in wide arcs, attempting to keep the discus at shoulder level.

Step Four: Teach the power position. Refer to the power position as described in the discus section. Have the athlete practice assuming the power position and pivoting on the right foot, keeping his weight over the right leg as he pivots the hips to the front.

    a.   As he pivots the hips to the front, "over-coach" the athlete to stay on the right foot so that when the hips face the front, he can pick the left foot up.

    b.   Next, have the athlete assume the power position using a light object, such as a shoe. Have him do standing throws, stressing that the throwing arm must be kept at shoulder level, performing an aggressive pivot of the right foot and a strong bracing of the left leg. He swings the arm back to the high point, then pulls the arm hard in a wide arc. When the "shoe" (discus) reaches the low point (six o'clock), the athlete drives the right hip forward against a braced left side. The hips must be pushed so that there is an arch in the long axis of the body (back). The feet should not be reversed.

    c.   After the athlete has "mastered" this drill, have him do the 180-Degree Drill, still with the shoe. He faces twelve o'clock with the left foot inside the back of the circle and the right foot outside the circle. He then drives to the center of the circle, landing on the ball of the right foot with the heel up, continuing to pivot on the right foot until he is in the power position, from where he tosses the shoe. Again, he does not reverse his feet.

    d.   The greatest fault at this point is the "shutting down" of the right foot by dropping the right heel. Have the athlete do a series of Wheel Drills. After the Wheel Drill, have the athlete do the 360-Degree Drill. He stands facing the direction of the throw. He swings the discus back and then does a 360-degree turn on the right foot. The athlete will finish in the power position and throw the discus or shoe. The coach stresses that the athlete stay on the ball of the foot with the heel high.

    Emphasis must be put on the left shoulder block, locked-out left leg, and a pivoting right foot and leg that blast the right hip forward. Do not allow the athlete to reverse the feet.

Step Five: The athlete now does standing throws with the discus without reversing his feet. He should

    a. Keep the right arm high.
    b. When discus reaches six o'clock, blast the right hip to the front.
    c. Keep the left leg locked, right leg straight at time of release.
    d. Have the discus flat at release, right thumb down.
    e. Block left arm and shoulder; do not let them move backward.

Step Six: Teaching the turn.

    a. Without a discus in his hand, the athlete is shown the proper position at the back of the circle. (See Starting Position discussion.)
    b. Have the athlete shift his weight to the left foot and pivot to the left on the ball of the left foot, keeping the left shoulder and arm over the foot until the foot points to three o'clock. Then have him pick up the right foot so that there is a 90-degree angle in the knee and do a 180-degree turn. When he can do this without losing his balance, have him progress to 360-degree turns. (A common error is to shift the weight to the outer edge of the foot.)

Step Seven: Three-Quarter Turn and throw.

    a. Have the athlete face the three o'clock position with the left foot inside the back of the circle and the right foot outside the circle about twelve inches behind the left foot.
    b. Have the athlete wind up and pivot the left foot to twelve o'clock, pick the right foot up and throw the right foot to the center of the circle, landing on the the ball of the foot. Have him continue pivoting on the foot until he lands in a well-balanced power position. The important points to emphasize are the throwing of the right foot to the center of the circle, aggressive rotation of the right foot, getting the left foot to the front of the circle as quickly as possible by tucking it under the hip, and a 90-degree relationship between it and the hips. When the athlete gets into the power position, he uses the same basic skills learned in Steps Four and Five.

Step Eight: When the athlete has "mastered" the Three-Quarter Turn Drill, the coach turns him to the rear so that he faces six o'clock. From this position, the athlete does the complete discus throw. This is where the real coaching takes place and the drills discussed in the Faults and Corrections section on the discus are used to help the athlete learn the different parts of the event.

SHOT PUT AND DISCUS

REFERENCES AND SUGGESTED READING

Altmeyer, Lothar. Wisconsin Track Coaches Association Track Clinic, Milwaukee, WI, 1993.

Ajan, Dr. Tamas and Baroga, Prof. Laza. *IWF Weightlifting: Fitness For All Sports.* Budapest: Medicina Publishing House, 1988.

Anderson, Lynne. Personal conversation at University of Minnesota. 1990.

Bartonietz, Klaus. Wisconsin Track Coaches Association Clinic, Milwaukee, WI, 1993.

Bondarchuk, Anatoliy. *Track And Field Training.* Kiev, Russia: Zdorovye, 1986.

Cappos, Scott. Personal consultation with Canadian National Shot Put Champion.

D and D Software, Inc. 146 21st Avenue, Vero Beach, FL 32962. 1992.

Doherty, Ken. *Track & field Ominibook,* 4th ed. Mountain View, CA: Tafnews Press, 1985.

Dominguez, Richard S. and Gajda, Robert S. *Total Body Training.* New York: Charles Scribner's Sons, 1982.

Dunn, George, Jr. "Developing The Young Shot Putter." *New Studies in Athletics.* March, 1990, pp. 35-43.

Dyson, Geoffrey. *Mechanics Of Athletics,* 7th ed. New York: Holmes & Meier, 1986.

Harre, Dr. Dietrich. *Principles Of Sports Training,* Berlin: Sportverlag, 1982.

Klatt, Lois A. "Specific Sports Skills Analysis." Monograph distributed at NSCA Convention, Orlando, 1989.

Krieger, Dieter. Wisconsin Track Coaches Association Clinic, Milwaukee, WI, 1993.

Modern Athlete and Coach, Jess Jarver, Editor. 1 Fox Avenue, Athelstone, S.A. 5076, Australia.

Nadori, Laszlo and Granek, Istvan. *Theoretical And Methodological Basis of Training Planning With Special Considerations Within A Microcycle,* Lincoln, NE: National Strength and Conditioning Association, 1989.

Payne, Howard. *Athletes In Action.* London: Pelham Books, Ltd., 1985.

Pedemonte, Jimmy. Personal correspondence, Genova, Italy, 1980-1987.

Poliquin, Charles. "Variety In Strength Training." *Sports Science Periodical On Research And Technology In Sport.* Coaching Association of Canada, August, 1988.

Poliquin, Charles. "Training for Improving Relative Strength." *Sports Science Periodical On Research And Technology In Sport.* Coaching Association of Canada, Vol. 1, No. 7, 1991.

Schmidtblelcher, D. "Strength Training, Part I: Classification Of Methods." *Sports Science Periodical On Research And Technology In Sport.* Coaching Association of Canada, August, 1985.

Schmidtblelcher, D. "Strength Training, Part II: Structural Analysis of Motor Strength Qualities And Its Application To Training." *Sports Science Periodical On Research And Technology In Sport.* Coaching Association of Canada, September, 1985.

Schmolinsky, Gerhardt, Chief Editor. *Track And Field,* 2nd ed. Berlin: Sportverlag, 1982.

Stevenson, W. (Stevie). "To Put (t) It Another Way." (Two part article) *Athletics Coach,* Year and month unknown, pp 16-20 and 20-30.

The Thrower, Max Jones, Editor. 152 London Road, Knowle, Solihull B93 9HU, England.

Tidow, Gunter. "Modern Technique Analysis Sheets For Throwing Events." *New Studies In Athletics,* March 1990, pp. 45-47.

Tidow, Gunter. "Aspects Of Strength Training In Athletics." *New Studies In Athletics,* January, 1990, pp. 93-110.

Track Technique, Kevin McGill, Editor. Track & Field News, 2570 El Camino Real, Suite 606, Mountain View, CA, 94040.

Tschiene, Peter. "The Throwing Events: Recent Trends In Technique And Training." *New Studies In Athletics,* March, 1988, pp. 7-17.

Tschiene, Peter. Ontario Track & Field Association Clinic, Toronto, Canada, 1976.

Verhoshanski, Y.V. *Fundamentals Of Special Strength Training In Sport.* Livonia, MI: Sportivny Press, 1986

Wilmore, Jack H. and Costill, David L. *Training For Sport And Activity,* 3rd ed. Dubuque, IA: William C. Brown Publishers, 1988.

HAMMER THROW

Yuriy Syedikh

HAMMER THROW

HISTORY

The hammer goes back a long time, all the way to about 2000 B.C. Historians record the throwing of stones, sledge hammers, and even chariot wheels with a single spoke attached. There is a well-known drawing of Henry VIII tossing a sledge hammer. Modern British royalty has stuck to swinging a polo mallet, which does resemble slightly the hammer used in the Scottish Highland Games: a wooden stick with a shot attached to the end.

Ireland was the early cradle of hammer throwing. From the ancient folk-hero Cuchulain down to the mid-1930s, Irish athletes, particularly Irish emigrants to the USA, dominated the event. Pat Ryan, a New York City policeman, set a record of 189'6" in 1913 which lasted for 25 years.

Among the great Irish whales were John Flanagan (three-time Olympic winner, 1900-1908); Matt McGrath (1912 gold, 1924 silver); Ryan, who won the Olympic championship in 1920, and Eire's Pat O'Callaghan (1928 and 1932 Olympic champion).

In the early days, the throw was accomplished off a dirt circle, and the athletes wore shoes with spikes in the ball of the foot. One or two jump turns were used, and this caused uncertainty as to where the hammer might land! This obviously put spectators and fellow competitors in peril. Unfortunately, there is still a great prejudice against the hammer in most areas of the USA, even though modern techniques and cages have made the event safe.

In the 1930s, German coach Sepp Christmann devised the heel/toe method of turning which enabled the thrower to keep at least one foot on the ground at all times. His throwers were dominant at the 1936 Games, and two years later Erwin Blask shattered the world record with a 193'7" throw.

Since the end of World War II, the world record has resided chiefly with Hungarians and the Soviet throwers. One deviation from this norm was the nine-year reign of the great American thrower Harold Connolly. Connolly won the 1956 Olympic Games hammer and set six world records from 1956 to 1965. His style was studied carefully by the Russians, who, since the 60s, have built an incredible string of throwers, culminating in the greatest duo of all time: Yuriy Syedikh and Sergey Litvinov. Syedikh, since 1976, has won two Olympic golds and a silver and has broken the world record four times. Litvinov has won one Olympic gold medal (1988) and one silver and set three world records.

Very few recent throwers in the USA have shown world class promise. Our 1988 Olympic trio of Ken Flax, Judd Logan and Lance Deal have been the cream of the US crop for the past few seasons, but there is still a 20-foot deficit to make up on the top Soviets. The USSR has more than 5,000 hammer throwers, while there may be 350 throwing in the USA, so we certainly have our work cut out for us. There is only one state where the hammer is an official event in the state high school meet: Rhode Island.

SPECIFICATIONS AND EQUIPMENT

Anyone seriously interested in the event must first concern himself with: where am I going to throw? You need a safe cage, placed far enough away from other events. The cage should be the same size as the IAAF-specified cage, with swinging gates in front which can be moved easily. Consult the IAAF and NCAA rule books for details.

Some schools allow throwing on multiple-use fields. It is important that someone fill in the holes!

Keep in mind, however, that if someone is in the line of fire and a throw takes place, no cage in the world will help. If attention is taken to safety, the hammer becomes a beautiful expression of rhythm, power, speed—unmatched in all of sport.

The hammer has three parts: (1) head or ball, (2) wire, (3) grip or handle. Inexpensive hammers consist of a solid iron head, although you can buy steel shells filled with lead, or other material. The filling in the shell should be immovable. The wires can be homemade from #11 piano wire, but the best ones are manufactured by the pros and currently cost around $6.00 each, to start. There are numerous handles available. Coaches should check the length and weight of the implements prior to meets, so there will be no surprises (deficiencies). Gloves with finger tips exposed, smooth front and back, may be used.

The hammer head must land inside the sector lines (40°). Where the handle hits is of no consequence. The rules state that you must continue the throw if the head hits the ground after the throw begins. It is a foul if you stop, but this rule has not been regularly enforced!

Other implements are contested: the 56-lb. weight; the 20-lb. weight for women; the 25-lb. weight for high school men; the 35-lb. weight for college and open men. The rules are the same for these events, as well as the basic technique. Just picking up a 56-lb. weight is enough exercise for most people! It is really a specialty event, not often contested.

THE PRINCIPLES OF THE HAMMER THROW

Since 1976, there has been a revolution in the hammer. Prior to that time, most throwers tended to use a "wound-up" or torque method in the event. This means that throwers attempted to gain a big lead on the hammer with the lower body. An attempt was made to gain a separation between the hips and shoulders, a crossing of the X, if you will, which would lead to a long pull at the end.

A modification of the older torque technique was used by the Polish athlete, Zdzislaw Kwasny, in the 1983 World Championships. He stunned the Russians with his 267'6" throw, which was taken away the next day by a Russian protest. Kwasny had fouled, but the Finnish judges did not call it. The 1984 Olympic hammer champ, Juha Tiainen, also used this technique, referred to by American coach Tom McDermott as "Drag City," because of the almost discus-like dragging of the hammer behind the thrower.

Not everyone is truly suited for the newer technique, which has been perfected by the Russians (even though each Russian has different quirks in his own style). Yuriy Syedikh is an example of the ball lead, catch-up style. Let's examine some of the reasons for his success.

Radius

The key to success in any throwing event is to increase the release velocity. That is the essential factor. Sam Felton's chart shows how a three-inch difference in radius makes a remarkable influence on distance:

IMPORTANCE OF A LONG EFFECTIVE HAMMER RADIUS
Thrower's turning speed (revolutions/second)
vs. different lengths in hammer's effective radius

Turning speed at instant of release (Revolutions/sec.)	Distance thrown (1) based on effective hammer radius (2) of—		
	6'0"	5'9"	5'6"
2.0	180'	166'	151'
2.1	200	186	168
2.2	220	203	185
2.3	240	221	203

(1) Based on 44° angle of release
(2) Distance from axis of rotation to about center of hammer-head.

Based on these figures, it may be estimated that Syedikh has an effective radius of greater than six feet, since a 286' throw would necessitate too high a turning speed. He is not turning much faster than a number of top throwers, he simply has an advantage in effective radius.

Range of Motion in Double Support

If you can extend the time you exert pressure on the ball force will increase. Syedikh is the master, as he lifts his right foot earlier each turn, and tries to get it down sooner for a greater range of motion in double support.

Mike Cairns has drawn a figure which shows the azimuthal angle of the hammer in double support. American coach Tom McDermott adds," Power comes from two feet on the ground. One cannot punch from one leg!"

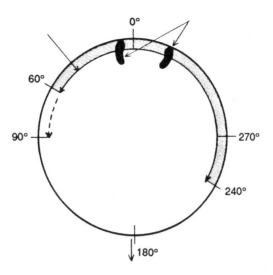

Hammer Orientation Diagram 0-360°

American hammer champion Dawn Ellerbe.

Free Leg Radius

This is defined as the distance between the center of gravity (c.g.) of the free leg and a line joining the base of the neck with the ankle of the support leg. This distance must be kept rather small, as it relates to the previous point, range of motion. The further your free leg is away from your body, the longer it will take to put it on the ground. The result is that you subtract time from when you can apply the greatest force on the hammer.

Length of each throw (L), speed of the hammer at the instant of takeoff of the right foot from the ground in turns 1-4 (SH_1-SH_4), speed of the hammer at release (SH_R), and angle formed by the horizontal plane and the hammer path at release (ANG_R).

Trial		L (m)	SH_1 (m/s)	SH_2 (m/s)	SH_3 (m/s)	SH_4 (m/s)	SH_R (m/s)	ANG_R (°)
Syedikh	10	80.46	17.7	22.6	25.1	----	29.1	42
	19	80.02	18.1	22.4	25.0	----	29.2	40
Litvinov	3	79.32	16.0	22.2	24.9	25.8	29.2	37
	12	ca. 80	17.0	22.6	25.2	26.5	29.5	37

Factors Which Determine Distance

The following chart shows the relationship between range or distance, release velocity, angle of release, and flight time of the hammer. Although other factors affect the hammer, such as height of release and aerodynamics, they are considered not very significant.

In the 1982 USA/USSR meet, Sergey Litvinov had a foul of about 80 meters which had a release velocity of 29.5 meters per second. The winning throw of 80.46 meters by Syedikh had a velocity of only 29.1. The difference was in the release angle. Litvinov's throw was released at 37 degrees, while Syedikh was perfect with a 42-degree angle. In this case, the release angle was crucial, but if you study the chart, you will see how an increase in release velocity can dramatically add to a throw.

AVERAGE FREE LEG RADIUS (FLR_1-FLR_4) IN THE SINGLE-SUPPORT PHASES OF TURNS 1-4 (IN METERS)

Trial		FLR_1	FLR_2	FLR_3	FLR_4
Syedikh	10	0.21	0.21	0.24	----
	19	0.21	0.20	0.24	----
Litvinov	3	0.18	0.20	0.19	0.22
	12	0.19	0.19	0.19	0.21

Tangential Velocity

Is the hammer pulled or pushed along its path? In the pre-1976 technique, the term was clearly "pull." Now, with the hammer being the leading element in the turn, we can think of the turn as a "unit turn," keeping the body as a unit, and pushing the hammer, utilizing the whole body, in relation with the ground. Syedikh's hips are barely ahead of the hammer, so it is clear that he can use his legs and hip power more effectively than the early techniques.

The thrower has to counteract the outward pull of the hammer, which is called the centrifugal force. By doing so, he maintains the proper orbit. However, it is only the combination of the horizontal forces and vertical forces applied on the hammer which will affect the tangential velocity. This is what the athlete must aim to maximize.

BASIC TECHNIQUE

The Grip

As in Figure 1, the athlete holds the hammer so that the handle goes across the end phalanges of the fingers on the gloved left hand. (If the athlete is a clockwise turner, or a "lefty", he will use the right hand.) The majority of throwers turn counter-clockwise and will "hold" with the left hand. The right hand will cover the left hand, as in the picture.

Figure 1

The Starting Position

Figure 2 shows the standard offset position for the hammer. There are many variations here, but the world record holder, Yuriy Syedikh, keeps it simple: place the hammer behind your right side, with the right arm, reach back with the gloved left hand, grip the hammer as shown in Figure 1, and you're ready to start.

Figure 2

Many throwers stand in an upright position and swing the ball into action without it ever touching the ground. This is an advanced technique which requires perhaps too much coordination for the beginner. It falls into the category of "nice to do, but not necessary."

When the thrower reaches back for the ball, his body weight will be centered over the right leg. This will help him lift the ball into position by straightening the leg, as he twists to the left.

Winds

The British call these "swings," but we will use the term "winds," as in windups. In these drawings of Sergey Litvinov, the sequence of movement is clearly shown. The thrower must SWEEP the ball to the front; CURL his left arm when the ball passes his body; then TWIST the shoulders to catch the ball beind him. Simply stated: SWEEP-CURL-TWIST. (Figure 3).

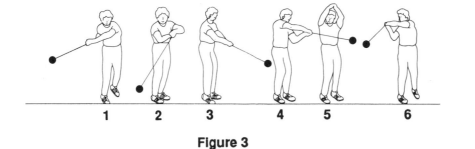

1   2   3   4   5   6

Figure 3

From Michel Thieurmel,
*Amicale Des Entraineurs
Française D'Athlétisme,*
#75, Dec. 1981.

The initial sweep of movement of the ball to the front is accompanied by some shifting of the body weight from the right leg to the left. However, there are no dramatic shifts in the center of gravity in the early stages, or the rhythm will be upset.

Since the body is bent over at the start, and the shoulders twisted to the right, as the thrower sweeps the ball around, the shoulders will unwind to face the front, and the arms will be straight out in front.

When the ball passes the thrower, he must concentrate on simply curling the left arm. This is the cue which will bring the hands close to the top of the head as the hammer passes behind him on the left side.

Keeping the body weight mostly central, the body twists the shoudler to "catch" the ball. SWEEP-CURL-TWIST. Be careful not to allow the right side to be soft and bend at this point. You want the right leg to remain perpendicular, and actually block the hip. The thrower should not let the hands pass beyond the center of the head (McDermott).

After one wind, the thrower repeats the sequence.

How many winds? Traditionally, only two, but there is no rule restricting you. More than three would be tiring! The winds are important in developing rhythm and balance in the throw.

Trajectory? A person using three turns must of necessity wind with a slightly steeper plane than the four turner. Note in Howard Payne's illustration (Figure 4) the plane for Syedikh was rather steep in the 1976 Olympics. As he still uses three turns, the hammer remains in about the same plane today.

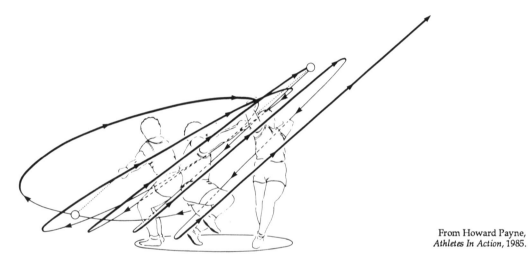

From Howard Payne,
Athletes In Action, 1985.

Figure 4: The changing tilt of the hammer plane during Yuri Syedikh's winning throw in the 1976 Olympics.

Low point? In the first wind the ball is kept off to the right to prevent creeping on the entry and in the turns. Ideally, you want the low point to be at zero degrees, or slightly left on the last turn.

Due to the differences in technical execution, what works for one thrower may not work for the next. Generally, keep the ball off the right leg, around 300 degrees on entry, and it will move to at least 0, or 360, by the last turn.

Some throwers have tried advanced ideas such as winding completely facing the right for the first wind, then stepping in. This complicates matters, and does nothing to improve distance. Others have tried stepping out a bit on the second wind to improve the base and prepare for the entry.

How fast? Some top throwers have actually gone too slow here in the USA. We don't see the Soviets in this country often enough to appreciate how quick Syedikh is in the winds. His ball moves like a blur into the entry. Some people concentrate so much on a slow entry that they never achieve decent release velocity.

The wind should be treated as part of the throw, not a separate event. As your ability to turn increases, so should your entry speed. Result: greater distance. In the beginning, however, the thrower must go slow to get accustomed to these strange movements.

Coach Tom McDermott has some thoughts about speed in the hammer which make a great deal of sense. In a November 1990 letter to the author he writes: "How fast? This is called *critical speed.* This is the essence of the athlete in the event. It's the speed he can handle. The better the athlete, the more critical speed he can handle. It is the difference between the champ and chump . . . and yet the coach should never mention the word 'speed.' He should stress only 'tempo' and 'cadence.' The speed will always be there—even more than most can handle. But also—don't extend the rump in order to 'let it out' for radius. Stay conformed, in body alignment with straight back. And a quick right foot."

The Soviets are expert at working the ball in the active (or descending) phase. They are very careful not to impede the ball's progress in the upward direction. In other words, they can leave the ball alone without pulling with the upper body. Perhaps this ability is due to differences in the societies, where the Soviets do not have baseball and football, but a lower body-oriented sport, such as soccer?

Entry or Transition

The entry actually begins at the high point of the last wind. The athlete must learn to lower his c.g. as he allows the ball to sweep to the front. When the ball is in front of the thrower, he must begin to apply force through a pushing action of the ball of the right foot, in association with an almost isometric-like action through the left heel.

The body should turn as a unit to the left. The thrower must get as much radius as possible on the left side and not be in a hurry to beat the hammer around with his lower body, as a discus thrower would. In other words, "Make haste slowly."

At the end of the second wind, the ball should "crack" out to the front and immediately out to the left. The stretching of both arms outward will form an isosceles triangle, which must be maintained throughout the whole throw.

In the past, some throwers attempted to pike at the waist to gain radius. Syedikh did this in 1975 when he threw in the U.S. However, his piking resulted in many people copying him and grinding their left foot into the ring as a result, not achieving his results. It was explained later that this "technique" we saw was an error resulting from a lack of strength! By keeping a straight back position, the thrower is in a much better position to control the hammer, and develop greater speed (Connolly).

When do you lift off the right foot? It is impossible to recommend an exact point when this should be done. No one could achieve it anyway. As a general rule, you must lift off before the hammer reaches 90 degrees for the first turn.

In subsequent turns, you should lift off slightly sooner than that. Syedikh was measured at 75, 60 and 55 degrees for his three liftoff points in 1982 by Jesús Dapena, on his best throw.

If you stay on the ground too long, it will be almost impossible to attain an early right foot placement at the end of the throw. Soviet Coach Anatoliy Bondarchuk made a statement in the early 1980's which indicated a later liftoff, but his throwers did not adhere to his words.

Turns

How fast do the top Soviets turn? Unless you are a speed reader, the best Russians can do three turns in less time that it took you to read the first line of this paragraph: under $1^1/_2$ seconds for three turns!

All throwers have to seek out the speed and the rhythm which suits them best. Although it is not uncommon to see throwers use four turns, Syedikh still uses three. If you can attain maximum speed with three, why use four?

Top throwers look for greater control on hammer acceleration, which is easier to attain with four turns. The feet turn in unison, with the left foot doing a heel-to-toe turn, with the right foot pivoting on the ball. The left foot usually begins turning when the ball approaches it in the entry, but this is an individual matter for the athlete.

The ball of the left foot is picked up, and the first 180 degrees of the turn will occur on the left heel and side of the shoe. Midway during the transfer from the heel to the ball, the weight will briefly pass on the outer edge of the shoe.

Prior to the hammer reaching the high point, the weight will have shifted to the ball of the left foot. In addition, the thrower will have lowered his c.g. to counteract the upward and outward pull of the hammer at the high point. The thrower's left knee will have maximum bend just at this point.

Remember, hammer high, thrower low. As the speed picks up the thrower may find himself leaning back to increase the counter, or displacement.

While all of these interesting things are happening with the left leg, what is the right leg doing? When the hammer is at 75 degrees, or before, the right foot should come off the ground in an active fashion. this is not a discus turn! There is a plantar flexion of the ankle joint, and a thrust using the large leg muscles. The top throwers even exhibit a brief heel kick like a sprinter, as this powerful plantar flexion of the ankle creates a "snap" of the right foot off the ground, up and over the left ankle and lower leg, and then quickly down to the ground.

The landing is on the ball of the right foot, which immediately gives the right leg a chance to apply another force. Some throwers have used a heel first landing, but this is rare and hard to master.

After the first turn, a thrower like Syedikh exerts so much pressure on the right side that you can see his leg muscles react to the force being applied through the leg and hip area. The placement of the leg must be very active, not quite a vicious stomp, but a powerful, active placing of the foot with an immediate potential to apply horizontal forces.

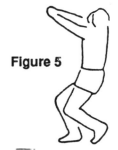

Figure 5

At this point, few athletes have been able to get the early landing of the right leg and the unusual hip position that the world record holder attains. Due to the incredibly fast placement of the right leg, Syedikh's hips are almost facing the ball. Even his left foot is just barely ahead of the hammer. Figure 5 shows this near-perfect position.

Drawing by Jesús Dapena.

Lance Deal, top American hammer thrower of the 90s.

Biomechanically, this is the most advanced technique in the world. No other thrower has quite reached this level.

Slower athletes may never achieve these positions due to the lack of quick reaction time. The famed German coach, Ernst Klement, explained that slower throwers must leave with the right foot even sooner than the faster throwers.

Syedikh has stated that he knows he has the ability to overtake the hammer at any time, but this is not the case with the rest of the world. Syedikh does not use a lower body lead on the hammer, and in fact, he gets farther back with the hammer on each turn on good throws.

This means that he leaves earlier, gets a good leg drive which rotates the thrower/hammer system rapidly, and has the time to catch the hammer earlier. This makes good, basic sense and is advice for any thrower regardless of throwing ability.

Delivery

TURN/LIFT. In the delivery, the thrower must continue to turn right to the last low point. Here, the hammer is lifted with a powerful extension of both legs, while the feet continue to turn.

Why are front squats important for top throwers? It is right here! As the legs lift, the upper body becomes more involved than at any time in the turns.

Some throwers use a braced left leg (it stops turning) which will cause the hips to stop also. Litvinov is the perfect example of this technique. Syedikh has gotten away from this in later years, not using a firm left leg block. The legs will straighten, the hips go forward, and the arms shoot overhead, all in one fluid, continuous, powerful action.

Immediately after release, the thrower must find a way to keep his balance by lowering the center of gravity, switching feet, or whatever, in order to avoid fouling. A blocked release simplifies matters!

Hal Connolly took the Olympic title in 1956, the last American to earn gold in the hammer.

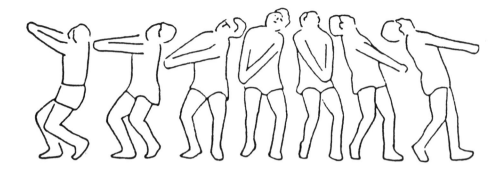

This drawing by Jesús Dapena, shows Yuri Syedikh delivering the ball on a 264' throw from the 1982 USSR/USA meet.

Summary

This sequence drawing by Jesús Dapena shows the major points of the throw. Even though we spent so much time breaking the throw down into parts, the lucky athlete who gets introduced to the hammer will find that many of these parts quickly flow together into a consummate blending whole.

Sequence of a hammer throw. The initial trajectory of the hammer after release (position v) is up and to the right in this drawing. The black and white horizontal bars indicate time intervals when both feet, and the left foot alone, respectively, are in contact with the ground. Each white-plus-black section indicates one turn.

FAULTS AND CORRECTIONS

WINDS

FAULT: The arms are pulled in, thus reducing radius.

REASON: The movements are tense; the thrower is inexperienced and he fears he will hit the ground with the ball, or be pulled off balance.

CORRECTION: a) practice with one-arm swings, left and right, using a lighter hammer and work for a complete range of motion;
    b) do regular winds with arms more relaxed (lighter ball) and correct stance until a wider sweep of the ball is possible. It is critical for the thrower to have the ball sweep across the front and wider to the left;
    c) build on an improved technique by using heavier hammers for a specific strength drill;
    d) stress a flatter plane, rather than a steep up-and-down motion.

FAULT: Low point is too far left or right.

REASON: Upper body is not guiding the ball correctly; winding speed is too high.

CORRECTION: a) *low point too far right.* The thrower must work the ball more to the left. He is bending his arms too soon as the ball nears the rear of the circle. He may have to lower the left shoulder more as the ball gets to the low point to enable him to sweep the ball a bit farther to the left;
    b) *low point too far left.* Thrower will have to curl in arms earlier and reduce the speed of the wind. He has not learned the wind rhythm yet.

FAULT: Body sways too much side to the side.

REASON: Athlete is attempting to put "more" into the wind by exaggerating the slight shift in bodyweight.

CORRECTION: a) keep body more upright throughout the wind. Don't swing the hips side to side;
    b) block with the right leg as the hammer begins to pass behind. Place heel firmly on the ground, and don't allow any sideways action of the right knee. Use a cue word: "Block."

FAULT: The hammer does not come up high enough to get into the proper plane.

REASON: Not enough initial acceleration. This is usually a beginner's error.

CORRECTION: a) practice a faster wind, but do not destroy the entry;
    b) do one-arm swings and heavy hammer swings for increased strength.

ENTRY

FAULT: The thrower loses balance in the turns.

REASON: a) started the turn with the shoulders and head;
    b) weight not on left leg, so it straightened;
    c) right leg did not drive into the turn;
    d) right leg lifted incorrectly;

e) thrower rushes upper body around and doesn't use hips and legs.

CORRECTION: a) bend legs at the end of the second wind, and sit back to counter the hammer at the low point;

b) keep left leg slightly bent and push the hammer through a wider radius;

c) do not lean too far forward;

d) make sure the center of gravity is near the left foot upon entry. This will come as a result of the above corrections;

e) keep the arms straight. Don't break the triangle after your arms extend at the end of the second wind;

f) beginning throwers may need the right foot on the ground to 90 degrees because they are not turning very fast. Better throwers will lift off earlier;

g) remember this is one of those faults which is common, but there may be any number of causes. Watch the athlete, study films, etc. to find the exact cause of the problem.

TURNS

FAULT: After the turn, the thrower "falls" onto the right leg.

REASON: As with the entry, left-shoulder, head and left-leg action and balance were incorrect. A wide swing of the right leg may occur.

CORRECTION: a) arms and shoulders must not pull in. Keep the eyes on the hammer, or rather have your face in the direction of the ball. When the ball hits the low point, you should not bend your neck to look at the ball;

b) keep the center of gravity near the left leg and get the hammer wide to the left. To do this you cannot straighten the left leg, tug with the shoulders, etc.;

c) keep the right foot in closer and be active in placing it on the ground. A delay will effect the whole throw.

FAULT: Smooth acceleration is lacking. Low rotation speed.

REASON: a) knees are bent too much at entry;

b) the thrower is bent over, overloading the left leg;

c) training may be improper, i.e., too much weight training;

d) improper leg drive.

CORRECTION: a) as you sit back to counter the hammer, straighten the leg a bit to increase the force and allow a faster entry. Don't exaggerate and stand up(!);

b) keep the back straighter, while relaxing the arms. A tight upper body may actually prevent your lower body from moving quickly;

c) get in better shape, and use lighter hammers in training.

FAULT: Thrower seems to turn in one spot.

REASON: Lack of countering at the low point.

CORRECTION: As the ball descends toward zero degrees, prepare to sit against the hammer quickly with the hips, while the back remains upright. Elite throwers do have some lean-back because of the much greater centrifugal force. The weight will move from the ball of the left foot to the heel during the aciton. This has to *happen*, not just be theory. Unless the force is directed opposite the hammer at the low point, you cannot overcome the hammer's force and move down the circle. If you lean forward you pitch the thrower/hammer c.g. system forward. Either you control this action. or the hammer will take over.

FAULT: Hammer hits the ground.

REASON: Trajectory is off.

CORRECTION: a) the thrower must not lean forward. He will lose the ability to control the downward path of the hammer;
b) winds may be too steep. Flatten them for correction;
c) make sure countering is correct.

FAULT: The right leg lands too far from the left leg, in a wide stance.

REASON: The thrower is using his upper body too much.

CORRECTION: Keep the left leg bent on entry and push hard with the right leg. Keep the right foot close to the left leg, so you appear to step over the left ankle. Put the right foot down with authority.

DELIVERY

FAULT: Too much weight on the right leg.

REASON: Upper body throw. Balance is off, causing this third turn problem.

CORRECTION: a) build specific strength using medicine ball throws against a wall; kettlebell work off a raised platform; one wind/delivery throws using heavy hammer on a short wire;
b) emphasize leg and hip during all drills.

FAULT: Upper body lean is excessive during the release.

REASON: Legs are straightened too early; the head is thrown back.

CORRECTION: a) work on maintaining good leg bend until the ball hits the low point. Drive up hard and feel "lift" as the ball rises;
b) get a good "drop" on the left leg prior to the right foot landing;
c) keep the head in a normal position and work on emphasizing an upward drive. Do the medicine ball drill against the wall.

FLIGHT OF HAMMER

FAULT: Hammer lands out of the sector.

REASON: a) left—over-completion of final turn; late landing; hammer jerked around by incorrect upper body action; legs straightened too early; head thrown back;
b) right—improper grip; low point way to the right; leaning forward causes loss of leverage.

CORRECTION: a) avoid straightening of the left leg going into the final turn. Don't rush the upper body around. Keep the right foot in tight, and aim for the earliest placement possible;
b) if gloves are worn, either replace or use chalk;

c) you should be bent at the legs, not the waist, as you land going into the final turn.

FAULT: Hammer flight is too low (rarely is it too high).

REASON: Either the winds were too flat or the turning action in the throw was incorrect. The trajectory of the ball should normally steepen on each turn. Tom McDermott suggests also that the arms may be tense, and the legs are not being used.

CORRECTION: If the winds are OK, correct the turns. There is usually not much of a drop against the ball at the high point, which causes the ball to slightly speed up and go lower.

(References: Ken Bosen, Harold Connolly, Jean Paul Baert, Gerhard Schmolinsky. See Hammer Bibliography, p. 96.)

TEACHING PROGRESSION FOR THE HAMMER

We need not have a long description of teaching the hammer. Why? Previous articles on the subject have had so many steps that the coach would either have to have a superb memory or he would have to stop many times to read the text.

Based on our experience at Level II, it is clear that a person can learn the basics of the throw very quickly, more quickly than the other three throws. The shot put glide requires some degree of practice to make it look right. The discus may be even more difficult because of the rotation involved. In less than fifteen minutes, however, a person can learn how to do two winds and two turns, plus a reasonable delivery.

Step One: We start with some hammer winds, and a basic delivery. Why? It is to get that young athlete hooked right off the bat. Also, you should use a very light hammer, or a medicine ball in a net. It is easy to swing a hammer around and let it go. Have the athlete use the proper grip, left hand on the handle first, right hand on top, if he turns left).

Put the hammer on the ground behind the athlete, and off to the right side. Have him pull the hammer off the ground, with an extension of bent legs, and get it going. As the hammer passes the left side, say "curl your left arm." This will get him into the right action.

Second, have the thrower concentrate on twisting the shoulders to the right as the hammer passes overhead.

Then, when he is winding, have him think "sweep" as the hammer comes forward and passes in front. Basic stuff: good balance on feet; arms loose—no pulling in; weight shifts a bit.

Finally, tell the athlete to let the hammer go as he does an about face with the feet to the left. It takes maybe three tries to get it right. If there is an up-and-down trajectory, the hammer will "fly." The coach need not get any more technical at this stage.

Step Two: The turns are more difficult. Get the thrower motivated and tell him he has just done two-thirds of the throw, the wind and delivery!

Place the weight on the ball of the left foot, and pick up the right foot. The left foot completes the turn, almost all the way around, and the right foot should be placed on the ground facing to the right, as in the illustration below.

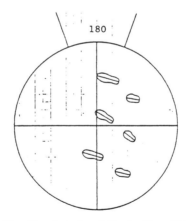

180

From Jesús Dapena, *Biomechanical Analysis Of Hammer Throw, #1,* USOC/TAC, July 1982.

The Footwork of Yuriy Syedikh

Step Three: After a few minutes of this practice, the athlete will be ready to try a turn holding the medicine ball in the net. Tell him to forget the ball is there and to keep his arms out in front of his chest. The ball will rise as the force increases. Repeat step two, but with the ball in hand.

Step Four: Now, the big test. Have the athlete wind the ball a few times to remember what was learned. When the ball passes the coach, who is standing in front (behind a fence, coach), the athlete is told to "turn." We are doing this *very slowly.* The slowest wind possible and a very slow turn. Repeat. After a few tries the athlete will get the idea. After two turns, there is usually a breakdown, so stick to two as the maximum for the first lesson. Tell the athlete: "Wind and let the ball turn you."

To summarize: two slow winds, two slow turns, and a delivery—practicing all the parts at once.

This is all that a beginner needs to work on for the time being. The rest can be added later. The more the athlete feels the process for himself, without constant correction, the faster progress will be. By incorporating the drills from the drill section, you can see a young athlete make amazing progress. Good luck!

Balázs Kiss, Hungary, 1996 Olympic champion.

HAMMER DRILLS

The coach with a creative mind can discover, or invent, dozens of hammer drills. You can practice turns holding just about anything in your hands. Some years ago, 1972 Olympian Al Schoterman used to put on street shoes and turn in a sandbox. Former American record holder Marty Engel hurt his left ankle in the 1960's and taught himself to throw over 170 feet in the reverse direction!! Instead of turning counterclockwise, Marty taught himself to turn clockwise. Bob Backus, another all-time American great in the hammer, had trouble with dragging the ball behind him. To correct this, he made a device which was hooked to his shoulders on one end, and it required Bob to bite down on a ball on the other end.

Perhaps the most creative minds in the hammer, as far as drills with innovative equipment are concerned, belonged to the duo of Gabor Simonyi and Rob Roeder. These two men wrote an article in *Hammer Notes* (#4, pp. 20-30, 1983?) which described combinations of boards, rubber cables, and bands connected in every which way, which when used judiciously, enabled the thrower to experience things with the hammer not felt before. In a more traditional vein, Stewart Togher, U.S. National Coach, has popularized a number of drills in his clinics that are also very useful.

BEGINNING DRILLS

In order to interest very young athletes in the hammer, it may be necessary to inject some fun. Italian coach Jimmy Pedemonte has used the following four drills to get youngsters involved in hammer activities:

Drill #1. Spinning with two partners. This may be done on the balls of the feet, as we are not concerned with exact technique here. The aim is to improve balance and rotary ability.

#1

Drill #2. Spinning with a medicine ball on a short handle. This somewhat resembles the 35-lb. weight, but the weight of this ball is much less. A medicine ball like this can be used by all young throwers.

#2

Drill #3. Spinning with a ball on a long rope. Even though this will go very slowly, the rotary ability gets a good workout. Again, for youngsters, keep them on their toes. Older kids can practice heel/toe turn on the left foot.

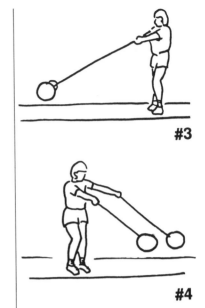

Drill #4. Spinning with two balls, on two separate ropes. By maintaining the position shown in the illustration, the young athlete will be learning advanced techniques, while having fun. With both arms straight out, as shown, the athlete is learning the proper relationship of the hammer to the upper body. Jimmy Pedemonte does this in large groups, and the kids love to spin around.

INTERMEDIATE DRILLS

As we progress to older youngsters and beginning throwers, we can recommend other drills which more closely approximate hammer technique.

Drill #5. Multiple turns with a stick. The thrower should concentrate on the heel/toe action of the left foot and the action on the ball of the right foot. Holding a piece of wood, as in the drawing, is fine, since it is light, and will keep the athlete's arms in front.

It takes a while to develop the ability to rotate more than five or six times without becoming dizzy, but this can be overcome. In the beginning, just do a few turns and stop.

Drill #6. Turns with a stick on the shoulders. This is a variation of the previous drill and is a good break for the athlete, since holding out one's arms can be tiring. Just constant turning, with the left foot turning 180° each time, and the weight shifting onto the ball of the left, keep it moving, and place the right foot down to the right, on the same plane as the left, but perhaps a little more off to the right, or tucked behind the left leg, as shown in the drawing.

Drill #7. Tug of war with a partner. This drill will give the young thrower the idea of balancing himself against the future increased pull of the actual hammer. This drill can be done by the athlete himself using a chainlink fence as a partner. With a partner, the advantage is that one person can "play" hammer, and the other can be the thrower. One tries then gradually to increase the pull. This is an enjoyable way to learn a major concept of hammer throwing.

Drill #8. Tie the ankles together with bicycle innertube or stretch cord. This is a good drill to teach the balance necessary in the hammer. Many beginning throwers "crash" on the right leg, and fall off balance—for a variety of reasons. By fastening the athlete's ankles together, you will make it easier for the athlete to experience the necessity of keeping some weight on the left leg at the end of the turn.

#8

Drill #9. Multiple winds. Up until now, we have concentrated on the turns in the drills. This drawing by Bjarke Dons, Danish National hammer coach, shows a young athlete in a complete wind.

There may be a little too much hip sway in picture 4, but this is a young person, and we won't be too critical!

As mentioned before, there are a few key words in the winds for cues: SWEEP-CURL-TWIST. It is very useful to repeat these words in instructing young athletes. Sweep the ball, curl the left arms as the ball passes the front of the left leg, and twist the shoulders to "catch" the hammer properly. This is also a good exercise for the out-of-shape coach!!!!!

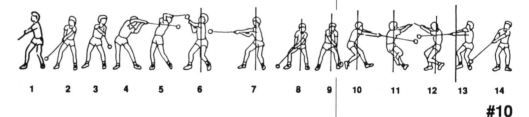

1   2   3   4   5   6   7

#9

Drill #10. Wind and turn. Have the young thrower wind twice, easy, and then turn, easy—stop. After a dozen repetitions of this, the athlete should be ready to go ahead with four or five continuous reps—all easy, with no concentration on increasing the ball speed.

World class athletes use this as one of their favorite drills. It is a good warmup exercise, as well as a teaching tool. You will find the young athlete having trouble with the ball speed, and he will miss the wind on occasion. Be patient, as there are many things happening here.

1   2   3   4   5   6   7   8   9   10   11   12   13   14

#10

Drill #11. Medicine ball deliveries. With the under-12 athlete, you will need a very light ball, 2 kg. or less. Juniors in high school can use up to 4 kg. for boys, 2-3 kg. for girls. Make sure the athlete can handle the ball easily.

Have the athlete stand next to a solid wall. Using the correct delivery action as shown in the illustration, have the athlete throw the ball into the wall, higher than his head.

In the beginning, just have the thrower catch it, stop, and repeat. An advanced drill is to have the athlete catch the ball, and then repeat the same drill over the other shoulder. This is one of the most important hammer drills ever devised. Top athletes take the 5 kg. ball and do many reps.

#11

ADVANCED DRILLS

There is some overlap in all of these drills. Some of the drills already discussed are used by advanced throwers. A few of the following drills are demonstrated in the Sybervision hammer tape, which is recommended for the advanced thrower.

Drill #12. Drills by Anatoliy Bondarchuk, the master hammer coach and Olympic champion from the USSR. Bondarchuk describes these exercises in his hammer text, which has only been available in Russian. This series of 25 drills contains many exercises which should be done only under close supervision by a coach.

You will notice that some of these drills involve the use of a bench for Russian twists. Please be careful to build up to these exercises, and do not have young athletes try all of these. This is really an advanced regimen.

#12

Drill #13. Throws with kettlebells. Unfortunately, kettlebells are hard to find in the U.S. This is another series of Soviet exercises to build specific hammer strength. If you cannot make a kettlebell, Obel in France may have them available. Shipping them here is expensive, but the die-hards will persevere.

The exercises: 1) left-arm tosses with bell, 2) two-arm tosses, 3) high pull to shoulder level only, 4) snatch as shown, to shoulder level only, 5) one-arm snatch, to shoulder level as shown. The Russians have various bells that they use, up to 15 kg.

#13

Drill #14. One-arm wind, with right or left hand. This is done slowly, and must mimic the correct pattern of the arm, as if two hands held the wire. The advanced athlete can then go into a turn and a delivery again at a slower tempo than normal.

#14

Drill #15. Declan Hegarty drills from the USSR. A few years ago, Hegarty, Irish record holder in the hammer, went to the Soviet Union and was shown these two drills by Oleg Kollodiy, a top Russian coach. The first drill is turning while holding a hammer in each hand. The second, is turning with one hammer, while holding the left wrist with the right hand.

#15

Drill #16. Plyometric drills. These must be done with great care. The interested coach should obtain Vern Gambetta's videotape from the NSCA for very detailed instructions on technique and on setting up a program for these drills.

#16

Drill #17. Short wire drills. Except for beginners, the use of the long wire has virtually disappeared. The Russians utilize the short wire for hammers as they increase in weight. Even the 15 kg. kettlebell is thrown off a very short wire. This is an absolutely terrific drill.

Drill #18. Four major lifts are used in the hammer. These are front squats, back squats, power clean, and power snatch. Other exercises, which would be considered assistance exercises for advanced throwers, can be used to build general strength in younger throwers.

It is not considered to be too helpful to include the bench press and curl to any great degree. Before 1976, prior to Syedikh's first Olympic title, it was more common to see hammer throwers utilize some bench press, since there was a greater concentration on throwing the 35-lb. weight. Since that time, we have learned that the Russians have succeeded in large part because they are hammer throwers first, and lifters second. The 35-lb. weight can almost be classified as a lift.

#18

From Esa Utriainen, *Keihaanheitto*, 1987.

HAMMER TRAINING

This will be a brief look at some specific hammer material, to supplement the "Training For Throwers" chapter. It is strongly recommended that the coach attend the Level I and II programs offered by The Athletics Congress (TAC/USA) to learn the principles of training theory.

We will take a look at a year-long basic outline devised by Soviet coach Anatoliy Bondarchuk.

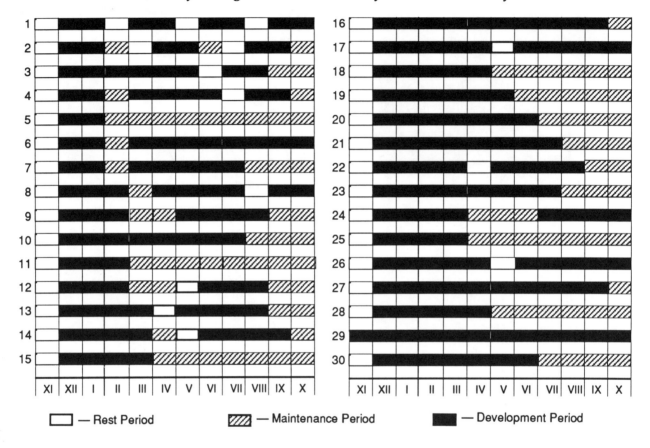

── Rest Period   ▨ ── Maintenance Period   ■ ── Development Period

The Annual Training Year by Anatoliy Bondarchuk.

The Roman numerals at the bottom of the charts refer to months, and they start with XI, or November. Reading down, you can see the emphasis for each day of the month. Rest periods for the Russians hardly ever means complete rest. The athlete usually engages in an alternative sport, such as soccer or tennis, and works on that for the period, as a type of recovery from the hard work of the previous year.

Notice that the competition period for the Soviets would be later than for the majority of American throwers. Bondarchuk tapers the work in the competition period, mixing in some easier days and even rest days. The major reason for studying a chart such as this is really to learn one thing: divide your training year into periods for optimal development.

The coach must take into account what level his athletes are at, how much time they can train, what facilities are available, and so on.

This particular outline is very rigorous. It is sometimes shocking to see the number of throws the Soviet hammer throwers have reported in a single year: up to 18,000 by a single thrower have been mentioned in some reports. Of course, that includes all types of throws, including ones with kettlebells, short wires, and so on.

The weightlifting and the throwing must be balanced and coordinated. A very heavy throwing session, followed by a heavy lifting session could literally bury a young athlete for a week. Using a common sense approach, the coach can steadily increase the amount of work the athlete does each year, which, all things being equal, will lead to longer throws.

SPECIFIC HAMMER TRAINING

If you have not already read the chapter on Training For Thowers in this book (p. 133ff.), please read it before you read this section. What follows is a discussion of training specifically for the hammer, and the assumption is made you have read the training chapter.

We realize this discussion applies more to the collegiate thrower or club athlete. The hammer is not widely contested at the high school level in the USA. Rhode Island is still the only source for the high school hammer, along with a small group in California. We wish the event were more widely held at this level.

HOW MANY TRAINING THROWS SHOULD I TAKE WITH THE HAMMER?

In discussions with coaches over the years, we find that volume varies greatly depending on the type of program the athlete is in. For instance, if the hammer thrower also is the shot/discus person for a small program, and is relied upon for team points, the amount of time devoted to the hammer will be minimal, well below the ideal for regular improvement. Thus, the question becomes only theoretical in this context, and the result is: the hammer loses.

Coaches tell us that they have their throwers throw all three heavy throws in a single workout. Perhaps this can work for shot/discus on the collegiate level, but if you want an athlete's hammer results to improve, he must specialize. The exceptions to this rule are very rare. The following answers therefore will be directed towards the specialists—the hammer throwers.

HOW MANY THROWS IN A SESSION?

In general, the answer will be between 10 and 40. This does not include standing throws or special throws. We do include throws with normal, light, or heavy hammers, though. Bondarchuk once pointed out that Litvinov needed more near-maximum throws than Sedykh in a workout, because Litvinov was rather high strung. Certainly, 40 hammer throws is an intensive and valuable workout, assuming attention was given to proper technical points. If the athlete is not 100% healthy, a low number may be fine, and for some a workout prior to a big meet might call for a low number of throws. Add 25-100 special throws, drills, etc.

WHAT INTENSITY SHOULD THESE THROWS BE?

The best answer, not a surprise, comes from Bondarchuk. His text, *Long Term Training for Throwers* (available through the Australian Track & Field Coaching Association), is remarkable for its clarity in answering this question.

We have combined Bondarchuk's "Zone of Intensity" chart with the percentage or the amount of throws he would have the thrower take in that zone. This simply means that only 10% of the throws will be taken in Zone 1, for example, and so forth. If my best throw is only 52 meters, how far do I throw? Table

Zone	%	% total throws
1	50-80	10
2	80-85	10-15
3	85-90	30-40
4	90-95	15-20
5	95-100	15-35

Table 1

2 explains the zone of intensity in meters, for each distance between 7 and 90 meters. Obviously, this chart will have a wide range for all throws.

Table 2 is an invaluable aid for the throws coach. No longer do you have to say, "Take a few 80% throws." You can state the exact range you would like, placing cones or marking some lines at the appropriate distances.

You may say, "Is this precision necessary?" Our answer to this is simple. Having studied the Russians since the early 1970's, the author is convinced that we need more precision in our approach to hammer training loads. This should never be left to a "Let's see what kind of day it is" attitude. Careful calculation over the years will give coaches the kind of data helpful in the future. While it is true that what works for one may not work for another, there is no question you will discover the path to greater hammer success by precise loading and careful record keeping.

Those familiar with the use of the computer may investigate Gary Winckler's "Training Design" program, which can be modified for use by the hammer coach. At present, there are really no other

100% (M)	95% (M)	90% (M)	85% (M)	80% (M)	50% (M)	100% (M)	95% (M)	90% (M)	85% (M)	80% (M)	50% (M)
90.00	85.50	81.00	76.50	72.00	45.00	47.00	44.65	43.30	40.00	37.60	23.50
89.00	83.60	80.10	75.65	71.20	44.50	46.00	43.70	42.40	39.15	36.80	23.00
88.00	82.65	79.20	74.80	70.40	44.00	45.00	42.85	41.50	38.30	36.30	22.00
87.00	81.70	78.30	73.95	69.60	43.50	44.00	41.90	40.60	37.45	35.20	21.50
86.00	80.75	77.40	73.10	68.80	43.00	43.00	40.95	39.70	36.50	34.40	21.00
85.00	79.80	76.50	72.25	68.00	42.50	42.00	40.00	38.80	35.65	33.60	20.50
83.00	78.85	75.60	71.40	67.20	42.00	41.00	39.05	37.90	34.80	32.80	20.00
82.00	77.90	74.70	70.55	66.40	41.50	40.00	38.10	37.00	33.95	32.00	20.00
82.00	76.95	73.80	69.70	65.60	41.00	39.00	37.15	36.10	33.10	31.20	19.50
81.00	76.00	72.90	68.85	64.80	40.50	38.00	36.20	35.20	32.25	30.40	19.00
80.00	75.05	72.00	68.00	64.00	40.00	37.00	35.25	34.30	31.40	29.60	18.50
79.00	74.10	71.10	67.15	63.20	39.50	36.00	34.30	33.40	30.55	28.80	18.00
78.00	73.15	70.20	66.30	62.40	39.00	35.00	33.35	32.50	29.70	28.00	17.50
77.00	72.20	69.30	65.45	61.60	38.50	34.00	32.40	31.60	28.85	27.20	17.00
76.00	71.25	68.40	64.60	60.80	38.00	33.00	31.45	30.70	28.00	26.40	16.50
75.00	70.30	67.50	63.75	60.00	37.50	32.00	30.50	29.70	27.15	25.60	16.00
74.00	69.35	66.60	62.90	59.20	37.00	31.00	29.55	28.80	26.30	24.80	15.50
73.00	68.40	65.70	62.05	58.40	36.50	30.00	28.50	27.90	25.45	24.00	15.00
72.00	67.45	64.80	61.20	57.60	36.00	29.00	27.55	27.00	24.60	23.20	14.50
71.00	66.50	63.90	60.35	56.80	35.50	28.00	26.60	26.10	23.75	22.40	14.00
70.00	65.55	63.00	59.50	56.00	35.00	27.00	25.65	25.20	22.90	21.60	13.50
69.00	64.60	62.10	58.65	55.20	34.50	26.00	24.70	24.40	22.10	20.80	13.00
68.00	63.65	61.20	57.80	54.40	34.00	25.00	23.75	22.50	21.25	20.00	12.50
67.00	62.70	61.30	56.95	53.60	33.50	24.00	22.80	21.60	20.40	19.20	12.00
65.00	61.75	59.50	55.25	52.00	32.50	23.00	21.85	20.70	19.55	18.40	11.50
64.00	60.80	58.60	54.40	51.20	32.00	22.00	20.90	19.80	18.70	17.60	11.00
63.00	59.85	57.70	53.55	50.40	31.50	21.00	19.95	18.90	17.75	16.80	10.50
62.00	58.90	56.80	52.70	49.60	31.00	20.00	19.00	18.00	16.80	16.00	10.00
61.00	57.95	55.90	51.85	48.80	30.50	19.00	18.05	17.10	15.95	15.20	9.50
60.00	57.00	55.00	51.00	48.00	30.00	18.00	17.10	16.20	15.10	14.40	9.00
59.00	56.05	54.10	50.20	47.20	29.50	17.00	16.15	15.30	14.25	13.60	8.50
58.00	55.10	53.20	49.35	46.40	29.00	16.00	15.20	14.40	13.40	12.80	8.00
57.00	54.15	52.30	48.50	45.60	28.50	15.00	14.25	13.50	12.55	12.00	7.50
56.00	53.20	51.40	47.65	44.80	28.00	14.00	13.30	12.60	11.70	11.20	7.00
55.00	52.25	50.50	46.80	44.00	27.50	13.00	12.35	11.70	10.85	10.40	6.50
54.00	51.30	49.60	45.95	43.20	27.00	12.00	11.40	10.80	10.00	9.60	6.00
53.00	50.35	48.70	45.10	42.40	26.50	11.00	10.45	9.90	9.15	8.80	5.50
52.00	49.40	47.80	44.25	41.60	26.00	10.00	9.50	9.00	8.30	8.00	5.00
51.00	48.45	46.90	43.40	40.80	25.50	9.00	8.55	8.10	7.45	7.20	4.50
50.00	47.50	46.00	42.55	40.00	25.00	8.00	7.60	7.20	6.60	6.40	4.00
49.00	46.55	45.10	41.70	39.20	24.50	7.00	6.65	6.30	5.75	5.60	3.50
48.00	45.60	44.20	40.85	38.40	24.00						

computer programs which allow modification, planning, and record keeping based on up-to-date knowledge of periodization, and the like. If one comes upon an early issue of the defunct publication, *Hammer Notes*, there is a story about Bondarchuk doing his record keeping and planning in the morning, and coaching in the afternoon. This is difficult to do with the demands on NCAA coaches and the incredible amount of time necessary for recruiting athletes. During a March, 1993 visit with javelin biomechanists and coaches in Kuortane, Finland, the author was pleased to note that Winckler's program was installed on the computer there.

WHAT ARE SOME SPECIAL EXERCISES FOR THE HAMMER?

Several are shown in the preceding pages. On a visit to Algeria in the mid-1980's, the author observed the African Champion, Hakim Toumi, run up a dirt hill using his right leg more than his left. He wore spikes and really emphasized the push on the right leg. He believed it helped him, and it probably did. Hakim also has a heavy, hollow kettlebell, purchased in France. It was like the item you see in Russian hammer drills—something like a 35-lb. weight, with a stiff handle. He threw this from every angle imaginable. Of course there was Russian coach in Algeria the year before, and Hakim had learned those drills from him.

On occasion, I believe some "intervention" with drills is a good idea. Greg Gassner, former thrower, has written an article on paradoxical coaching in the hammer. He believes that you can coach an athlete to keep his arms out. . . by telling the athlete to try to pull them way in!* The athlete soon finds out it is easier to keep them out.

If the athlete insists on a straight left leg, simply tie a strong band between the left heel and a weight belt around the waist. As the athlete goes into single support, the band will assist in "pulling" the athlete down.

Years ago, we tried really long hammers, about one foot or more longer than normal. Wow, did that increase the force. But, it was much too slow and we abandoned that idea. Today, lighter hammers are crucial in training, and the trend has been to stay away from those longer hammers. What weights should be thrown? Bondarchuk had two slightly different lists for throwing with the competitive movement and then for various supplementary exercises:

Weights for Competitive Movement
4, 5, 6, 6.5, 7.25, 8, 8.5, 9, 9.5, 10, 11, 12, 13, 14, 15, 16—all in kilograms.

Weights for Supplementary Exercises
2, 3, 4, 5, 6, 7.25, 8, 9, 10, 11, 12, 13, 14, 15, 16, 24, 32—all in kilograms.

Unfortunately, these weights were only listed for men, since women did not throw the hammer often in Russia. Currently, in the USA, women's hammer throwing is spreading widely—an excellent sign for all throwers. Coaches dealing with the women's hammer can get the idea from this list, and extrapolate from the 4kg weight.

There is no secret to the list, as Bondarchuk described in earlier writings how he tried many different combinations of light, heavy, and normal to achieve success. The exact prescription is made by the coach, in consultation with the athlete, as to the actual weights thrown in workouts.

The general rule of thumb has been: heavy emphasis in the fall and early winter, with a shift towards lighter in spring. There is no way a thrower can develop speed by competing and throwing the 35-lb. weight or 20-lb. weight (for women) all winter. In the Northeast USA, the indoor season begins the first week in December and does not end until the first week in March. For a hammer thrower to begin actual hammer work then could be disastrous.

CONCLUSION

The hammer is not much different than any other event in track. American coaches start throwers later than in Europe, and the tremendous effort needed to master the hammer is difficult for both NCAA athlete and coach. Few coaches have the luxury of specializing in the hammer alone, and the American athlete is hard pressed to find the time to reach the heights more easily attained by foreign throwers, almost every year, in NCAA Division I.

---

*This article will appear in *Track Technique*, No. 129, Fall 1994.

HAMMER THROW REFERENCES AND SUGGESTED READING

1. Baert, Jean Paul. *The Throws*. Ottawa: Canadian Track and Field Association, 1980.

2. Bertram, Alan. "A Visit to the Soviet Hamer Training Camp." *Track Technique*. No. 122. Winter 1993.

3. Bondarchuk, Anatoliy. *Hammer Throw*. Moscow, 1985.

4. Bondarchuk, Anatoliy. *Long Term Training for Throwers*. Available from Australian Track & Field Coaching Assn. and Rothman's Foundation. 1992.

5. Bosen, Ken. *Training and Teaching Throws*. Patiala, India, 1985.

6. Connolly, Harold, 1988. "What Makes Syedikh's Technique So Effective?" *Track Technique*. No. 102, pp. 3260.

7. Cairns, Mike, 1981. "Basic Points of Hammer Technique," *Track and Field Quarterly Review*. Volume 81, No. 1, p. 42.

8. Dapena, Jesús, et al. *Report For Elite Athlete Project, Biomechanical Analysis of Hammer Throws*. Amherst: USOC, July 1982.

9. Doherty, Ken. *Track & Field Omnibook*. 4th edition. Los Altos: Tafnews Press, 1985.

10. Dons, Bjarke. "Hammer Test," *Hammer Throw*. Denmark, 1988.

11. Felton, Sam and Simonyi, Gabor. *Modern Hammer Technique*. Rosemont, Pa., 1979.

12. Hegarty, Declan, 1985. "Hammer Throw," *Hammer Notes #9*, pp. 46-55.

13. Hoff, Anders. "Hammerkast-simplere end du tror," *Mjolner*. #3, pp. 12-13.

14. Jaede, Eberhard. "The Main Elements of Modern Hammer Technique." *Track Technique*. No. 118. Winter 1991.

15. Jones, Max. *How to Teach the Throws*. London: BAAB, 1986.

16. Payne, Howard. *The Science of Track and Field Athletics*. London: Pelham Books, 1981.

17. Pedemonte, Jimmy. *Hammer Notes #1-9*, New York, 1981-85.

18. Roy, Jacques, 1981. "Le Marteau," *Revue de l'AEFA* #75, pp. 36-53.

19. Schmolinsky, Gerhard. *Track and Field*. Berlin: Sportverlag Berlin, 1983.

20. Utriainen, Esa. *Keihaanheitto*. Helsinki: Suomen Urheilulitto, 1987.

21. Winckler, Gary. *Training Design 6.0*. (Computer Software). Available from M-F Athletic Company, Box 8090, Cranston, RI 02920. Tel. 1-800-556-7464.

JAVELIN THROW

Petra Felke

JAVELIN THROW

HISTORY

Javelin throwing is probably as old as mankind. In hunting cultures, if you wanted to eat, you had to make a spear and practice throwing it. And of course the spear was useful in defending the clan against hostile attack.

A few years ago, I watched a TV show about the Australian aborigine. One native held a thin, wooden stick about five feet long, to which was attached a thong at the end. The thong was wrapped about his wrist. He approached a small clearing, holding the spear over his head with the tip pointed down. Suddenly a small animal appeared and, in an instant, he delivered that spear unerringly into the animal's side. For a few minutes, the viewer was brought back into prehistory when spear throwing was essential for survival.

At some point in time, people started to use spear throwing in forms of competition. Perhaps they threw heavy spears to show their strength? Accuracy, though, was probably the most common goal in these competitions, rather than length.

The early history of the javelin in track and field competition is essentially Scandinavian. Only Finns and Swedes held the world record until 1953 when American Franklin "Bud" Held shocked the athletics world with the first 80-meter throw (80.41/263'10").

Of those early Scandinavian throwers the three most prominent were Erik Lemming of Sweden and Jonni Myyrä and Matti Järvinen of Finland. Lemming was the pioneer stylist of the event. He won the first two Olympic javelin competitions (1908 and 1912). The two great Finnish javelinists exceeded the world record 18 times, though Myyrä actually was only credited with one official record by the IAAF. He did win two Olympic titles, however (1920 and 1924).

Järvinen is considered the greatest javelin thrower ever. He broke the world record 11 times (1930-36) and won the 1932 Olympic championship. A back injury held him to fifth place in 1936.

The Finnish tradition of javelin throwing continues today; the winner of the 1990 European Championships in the women's javelin was Päiva Alafrantti. The event is still probably the most popular event in the track and field program in Finland.

Americans were held back for some time due to the American "hop," in contrast to the Finnish crossover technique (popularized by Järvinen). After Held's record throwing, helped by his experimentation and improvement of the implement itself, another breakthrough for the Americans was the 282'3 1/2" record throw by Al Cantello. Cantello, who was only 5'7", 165 lbs., used a technique which incorporated a "flying release" in which he left his feet after the release, diving forward and landing on his hands.

By the time Germany's Uwe Hohn sent a "glider" out to the astounding distance of 343'10" in 1984, the IAAF rulemakers decided that the javelin had to be modified to keep it in the stadium. The center of gravity of the implement was moved forward and other alterations were made to limit throwing distances.

As the record for the "new" javelin hovers around 300 feet at this writing, it's a question of whether enough changes were made. It looks as though this expensive move by the IAAF will have as much effect as the change in the hammer diameter a few years ago. The hammer record has continued to soar despite the change.

The first truly great women javelin thrower was Germany's Ruth Fuchs. A two-time Olympic champion (1972 and 1976) and six-time world record breaker, she just missed becoming the first female 70-meter thrower. She was succeeded in Germany by another magnificent thrower, Petra Felke, who has surpassed the world record four times, her last great throw hitting precisely at 80 meters (262'5") in 1988. She won the Olympic title in 1988, but has been thwarted in other big meets by her rivals from Britain, Fatima Whitbread and Tessa Sanderson. Tiina Lillak from Finland, the 1983 World Champion, twice had world record throws in the early 80s.

American women have not kept to the pace set by the 1977 world record throw of Kate Schmidt (227'5"). Karin Smith is a fine technician and has had a long career and is the best U.S. female javelinist of the 80s. The U.S. scene is not terribly encouraging. Karin, at age 35, still led the U.S. list in 1990 and was more than 20 feet behind the best international marks. Only one other American thrower, Donna Mayhew—another veteran—exceeded 200 feet.

SPECIFICATIONS AND EQUIPMENT

Modern throwing is usually conducted on the same artificial surface track meets are held on. Since these surfaces are harder and not as forgiving as grass, knee injuries have been more frequent. Athletes are advised that they should take out most of the spikes in their drive leg (right leg for righties), to allow a quick pivot without damage to the right knee. The 1988 Olympic Trials in Indianapolis was the largest gathering of knee braces ever seen at a track meet!

In the construction of an artificial runway, be sure to follow a few simple steps: (1) allow at least one extra meter beyond the painted foul line; (2) brush off any excess granules before practice or competition or it will be like throwing on ball bearings; (3) check that throwers have the correct length spikes, as some throwers feel they must put longer spikes in to get a good bite. This can lead to injury.

The landing area must be away from all other events. A good javelin thrower can send a javelin up there for several seconds—time enough for an oblivious athlete or official to wander into the area. Be careful to rope off the area when throwing takes place.

Javelin selection is getting difficult for high school boys who search for old-style javelins. Some are still being made; you just have to look for them. Also, for the high school thrower, rubber tipped javelins are available in men's and women's models. While they will not fly as far, the rubber tipped javelin may be the only thing which will save the javelin in many states. If your state does not have javelin as an event, why not purchase one, and bring it around so people who make these rules banning events can be educated? There is no reason to ban the javelin! They would be better off banning teenage driving if the real goal is to save lives. "Throw The Javelin; Don't Drive!!"

High school boys have a choice of beginner's javelins, short, medium, long, and even elite. Only selected Sandvik javelins come with rubber tips, while all Held and OTC javelins can come with tips. High school women have a wide choice available, rubber tipped or regular. Since the range is from 30 meters to over 70 meters, it is important to realize one thing: while it may be true in some wind conditions that you can throw a higher rated javelin farther, be prepared for flat throws. If you want consistent calls in college and open competition, you should learn how to flight a javelin for a point first landing. College *men* do not have this problem, as they are throwing a new rules javelin, which will stick anyway you throw it.

Open men have one major problem right now. The cost of the better Sandvik javelins is getting prohibitive. At the time of this writing, the top rated Sandvik model is over $450. Adidas javelin boots have also gone through the roof. Either you, your school, or club, will have to make some difficult decisions about what equipment to buy. When a few javelins, and a pair of spikes can run you over $1200, it is difficult to explain to an athletic director.

M-F Athletic also sells lots of training aids for the javelinist: nockenballs, medicine balls, cables, weighted balls, medicine balls with holes for ropes, etc. One essential tool is a copy of Dr. Robert Sing's *The Dynamics of the Javelin Throw.* Dr. Sing is an osteopathic physician by profession, a javelin authority by avocation, and he has helped out hundreds of throwers and coaches throughout the world. His book is one of the few classics in track literature.

JAVELIN TECHNIQUE

The javelin has seen three important developments over the past 20 years: (1) the wrap, or rotational style of throwing, (2) the change in the men's implement in 1986, (3) the development of the active right leg, or scissor style. Absolute answers on some of the technical points to be discussed cannot be given, because what works for one may not work for another. The variety of styles in the javelin is one of the aspects which has made the event so interesting to coach.

THE GRIP

While the Finnish grip shown in Figure 1 may be the preferred style for most, 1983 World Champion Tiina Lillak utilized a variation in one sequence where she slid her hand down the shaft, with the thumb and second finger in the middle of the javelin cord. She maintained her index finger behind the edge of the cord.

Former world record holder Tom Petranoff stated in his video on the javelin that he now prefers the fork grip.

The issue concerning rotation of the javelin with the Finnish grip vs. lack of rotation with the fork grip is not over. In a 1983 biomechanics film, investigators found that the javelin rotates nearly 25 times/second. But . . . this is with the old javelin. Canadian coach Jean Paul Baert wrote in his book on the throws that the Finns discovered that the thumb and middle finger are the strongest fingers in the hand, and this favors the Finnish grip.

Frankly, it boils down for most throwers to comfort and consistency. It appears that the Finnish grip may have an advantage in giving the thrower a more consistent flight.

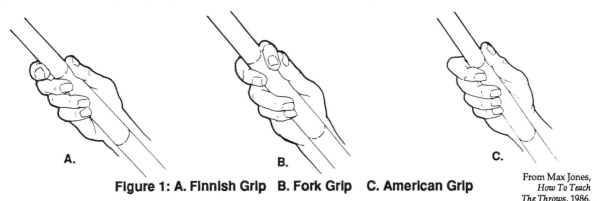

Figure 1: A. Finnish Grip B. Fork Grip C. American Grip

From Max Jones,
*How To Teach
The Throws*, 1986.

THE CARRY

The horizontal, over-the-shoulder position, is clearly the most popular, as it allows an easier withdrawal motion of the javelin. Many throwers, however, like to keep the point down during the carry. This is not a point of major concern. Holding the javelin way up, as some do, does nothing but create tension in the shoulder.

APPROACH RUN

Observation of top throwers at major international events will demonstrate that the number of strides in the runup can vary according to the number of throwers. Ten strides is a good average number, however. Finnish recordman Jorma Kinnunen used to fly to the line with *16 strides*.

What is of concern is how slow the runups have become in recent years for American throwers. The general routine is: jog a few steps, withdraw, accelerate a bit, and then gun it.

Ten steps allow the thrower to build into the run, without the quick, last-second tense moves, which are now common. The beginner should start with fewer steps, however.

The great Polish thrower Janusz Sidlo once told Milt Sonsky, a 1972 American Olympian, that the athlete must be relaxed in the run, right up until the final effort.

You need two check marks: (1) start of the run, (2) start of the withdrawal of the javelin. Early on, the thrower must learn one lesson: fouls do not count. It is only by repeated runway work that the thrower will make the run automatic enough to avoid the fear of fouling and enable him to concentrate on throwing.

Figure 2: The Runway Steps.

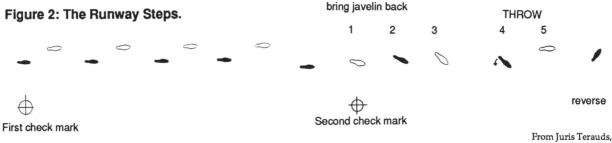

From Juris Terauds,
Biomechanics Of The Javelin Throw, 1985.

WITHDRAWAL

As we have more than implied, much of javelin technique involves choices and variety, rather than hard-and-fast rules. It is here that we run into problems with the withdrawal, which marks the beginning of the more or less intricate step pattern in the javelin throw. Before we discuss the mechanics of the withdrawal, it is proper to bring up the rhythm of the throw, which is critical to succeed.

As the right handed thrower hits his mark for withdrawal, he will begin the step pattern of the javelin. There is a decided rhythm to these climactic steps:

One—Two—Three—Four—Five, or Left—Right—Left—Right—Left. If you are not familiar with this rhythm, why not stand up right now where you are reading. Move your left foot up on "One", place it down, pick up your right on "Two", etc., and so forth. As you are copying the written rhythm, you may have noticed that the spaces are shorter between the final right-left. This is the heart of the throw. This must be practiced!

As you hit the first of the steps, which will be with the left foot, you will withdraw the javelin, or as some coaches have stated, run away from the javelin. It is like leaving the javelin in space, as you continue to run. A straight pullback is advised, and is shown in the figure below:

Figure 3: The Withdrawal.

From L.S. Khomenkova,
*A Textbook For The Track
& Field Coach*, 1982.

Those familiar with javelin history are aware of other methods that have been employed: (1) "front side drop," (2) slight "side drop," (3) underhand carry. None have any advantages; they only succeed in making the throw complicated.

The withdrawal can be completed in one step. As the left arm comes forward in a natural running motion, along with the right leg, it is a simple matter to have the javelin in position with a minimum of effort.

Figure 4: Overhead View of Steps.

It is important to keep the second foot placement, the right foot, in line with the throw. This is rather hard at the beginning, since the thrower is turning his upper torso to the right in the withdrawal. The coach must make sure that the right foot is in position, which will allow the right leg to maintain the correct rhythm in the steps.

Hip position is a variable based on your flexibility, and your choice of style. For orientation, we will say that if the hips completely face the right side, they are 90 degrees out of the line of the throw. Hips 50% more to the front will be at 45 degrees, and so forth.

Generally, there have been actually five different positions noted in throwing history: (1) more than 90°, as in Bud Held, (2) 90°, as with Tom Petranoff and other wrappers, (3) the three-quarter position, or 60°, as with Hungarian Ferenc Paragi, who broke the world record in 1980, (4) half side, or 45°, the most popular, (5) front facing, as with Miklos Nemeth's coach, Gergely Kulcsar. The 45-degree position allows for the most favorable combination of application of force, and continuance of running rhythm. The hip also is compared to the shoulder, and in this comparison we have observed only two positions with the shoulders: (1) more than 90°, as with Petranoff, and (2) 90°, as with the vast majority of throwers. This relationship refers to the principle of torque, which is discussed in the chapter on Basic Principles.

ROTATION OR WRAP VS. LINEAR THROW

With big throws being produced by both styles, it is difficult to make a definite judgment. However, the "J" action of the rotational thrower is sometimes tough to defend. When Petranoff won his first TAC championship in 1985, he threw a number of throws outside the sector on the right side that might have won it earlier for him.

Due to the "reach back farther and nail it" philosophy, Petranoff's left foot was in line with his right during the actual throw, or even to the left side—which produced blocking in his hips, an error. By moving his left leg over a bit in the plant, he was able to produce the winning throw.

Is the additional 12-18 inches of "pull" on the javelin worth the effort? We vote "no." The reason goes back to simple biomechanical analysis. The "pull" one sees in the rotational throw is misleading. While there is some contribution given to the throw prior to the landing of the left leg, it has been noted that the hand of the thrower moves almost to the identical relative position of the linear thrower at the plant of the left foot.

The problem in so many films of throwers is a simple one: the javelin is out of line in rotational throwers, moreso than with linear efforts. If this problem can be worked out, the potential for improvement still exists. In theory, it works, but in practice . . . Experiment on your own; research it.

The biggest problem with a rotational style may be the doctor bills resulting from injuries, primarily to the knee. Hard rubberized tracks are the enemy of the javelin thrower.

THE CROSS STEP

This phase is also called the pre-throwing stride. There has been a recent development in this area, which bears looking into. Due to the influence of Jan Zelezny, one of the most successful of the new rules javelin throwers, coaches have been discussing another approach, which we will call the "right leg scissor" technique.

**World record holder
Jan Zelezny.**

After the thrower withdraws the javelin, he will be on his right leg. Continuing his drive, as in the earlier overhead drawing of the steps, the thrower must place his left leg, the third count, in position for the pre-throwing stride. By keeping a low, powerful, forward action, the thrower is now ready for the crucial step in the whole throw.

Two choices: (1) the passive right leg. This doesn't mean the leg is totally useless, but it does refer to the older style of simply getting into position on a bent leg, with no backward, pawing action, etc.; (2) the scissor, or active right leg. This is what Zelezny and others are doing. Instead of waiting for the ground contact, the thrower drives forward in almost the same fashion as in the other style, but simply brings the right foot back, in a powerful, pawing action. It is like a jump or hop back and paw action.

Now, there are problems with this action. Some top throwers (Zelezny among them) have encountered back problems. Zelezny now wears a weight belt. Tommi Viskari from Finland, who holds the U.S. high school record for the new rules javelin, also uses this technique, and his progress has been slowed by back problems. It is a relatively new technique, and we don't yet know what effect it has on the back.

Why do the scissor? It puts the left foot on the ground very quickly. The rhythm of the throw is very fast at the end. You may subtract some range of motion, but the gain, if we look at Zelezny, may be substantial. The thrower arrives into the throwing position faster, relatively, than the older technique.

Can all throwers scissor? Probably not, and they shouldn't. The reason is that this technique requires very fast reflexes. Some average throwers will spend more time trying to do this, and must be on their left leg before they think of throwing. The coach must test which athletes can handle what: it boils down to the coach's judgment.

The biggest problem which scissoring solves is in Figure 5 below, the slow left leg. You can fix this problem with either technique, and it bears a good look. The left foot should be out in front of the right at this point.

Figure 5: The Slow Left Leg.

From *Dyson's Mechanics Of Athletics*, 1987.

You must get the left leg down fast in the javelin. That is the ticket for success. If the left leg takes a long time to get down, the throw is lost. Blocking is impossible, as there will be no gain, since the weight will shift to the left too soon.

Causes for a slow left leg are many. A common one is the 90-degree placment of the right foot in the throwing stride, which literally blocks the thrower's momentum. This is seen in many, many throwers. The placement of the right leg in the 45-degree position will help.

The ideal throwing action starts off the right foot, not the left. Why is this? There is clear biomechanical evidence, and in film analysis, that the right leg is a non-contributor to the throw shortly after left foot contact.

The right leg is active earlier for a good reason. One of the effects in the throwing process is the stretch across the upper body, resulting from a good blocking action on the left side. The thrower must be careful not to rotate his left foot out too far as a result, but the attempt must be made to engage the rotation of the lower body to increase the potential for a stretch reflex—the unwinding of the upper body, speeded up by a good X position between hips and shoulders. The left arm is long, to delay the rotation of the upper body.

In summary, the right leg drives the hip forward, but after left foot placement, it will primarily be the blocking action of the left side which will complete the hip rotation.

THE THROW

In the series illustrated below, the thrower is using a wrap style with a forward facing right leg—very advanced! A study of the film from which this is taken showed that the javelin had almost come into line

107

when the left foot landed. Notice the throwing action itself with the right arm. Right palm is up, the elbow leading, the rotation after release, thumb down—this is superb technique.

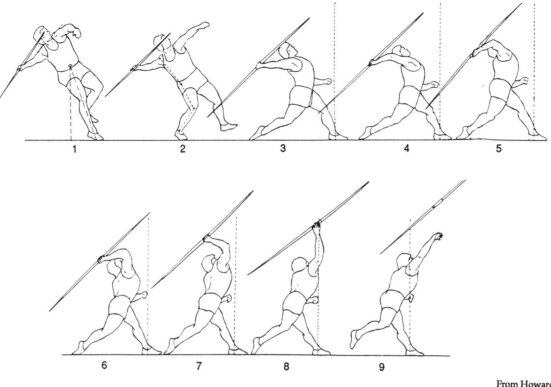

Figure 6: Throw by Ferenc Paragi.

From Howard Payne,
Athletes In Action, 1985.

The throw below features many advanced technical points. Figure 7 shows a thrower with a very slow left leg plant, a soft left leg and a poor block, among the negative features!

Figure 7: The Wrong Way!

From *Dyson's Mechanics Of Athletics*, 1987.

The left arm used in the Paragi illustration goes backward/downward, helping in the blocking action of the left side. The quick placement of the left leg, an absolute must in any style, should take place almost on the flat of the foot, with perhaps the heel strike first.

The soft, bent leg, which was experimented with years ago, has vanished from the scene. We now see a real BLOCK in to throwing, where the attempt is made to stop the left side and accelerate the right side.

In the rotation of the right leg, be extra careful to have the thrower remove most of the spikes in the right shoe. This to enable a fast rotation, without damage to the knee.

Pulling with the arm, a very common error in high school javelin throwing, comes from our culture, from our baseball and football experiences. We are "throwers", and we must learn to delay the arm in order to take advantage of these various forces at work which will create a much, much longer javelin throw.

The resulting arch position, the reverse "C" (#3 in the Paragi series), is typical of good throwing. It is biomechanically sound: arm delay, big muscle groups first, small groups second, etc. It is a simultaneous chain reaction happening in a split second.

Former American record holder Tom Petranoff delivers the javelin.

JAVELIN FLIGHT FAULTS, CAUSES AND CORRECTIONS

FAULTS	COMMON CAUSES	CORRECTIONS
TRAJECTORY TOO STEEP Short flight Marked nose-dive	— Thrower fails to adequately drive over the front leg at delivery. — Point up misalignment during withdrawal. — Power applied vertically rather than "through the point of the javelin." — Throwing arm gets ahead of the final action of the trunk.	— Correct the placement of the front leg and its braking action. — Practice supporting the javelin in the throwing hand during withdrawal and cross-over. — Practice correct withdrawal. — Simulation drills using slingballs, shot and javelin thrown two-handed from behind the head — standing, off three strides, and from a run. — High chopping with a handaxe. — Easy standing throws, and throws from a short approach.
TRAJECTORY TOO LOW	— Incorrect rhythm in the approach run. — Lack of necessary mobility. — Lack of coordination. — Lateness in timing the delivery.	— Practice approach runs, and cross-overs. — Increase the amount of mobility and conditioning work. — Simulation drills involving use of legs and hips to achieve "bow" position at delivery. — Simulation drills delaying arm action until legs and hips have done their work. — Easy throws working on aspects of both sets of simulation drills.
NOSE UP Produces stall Short flight	— Slackened grip on javelin. — Slack throwing wrist causing its HYPER-EXTENSION. — Lowering of throwing hand/arm. — The final throwing effort does not go "through the point." — Last stride too long. — Front leg flexed, or allowed to collapse.	— Correction of grip, and wrist tensions. — Repeated withdrawals maintaining high hand—standing, walkup, running with cross-step. — Proper location of checkmark. — Simulations of corrected front leg activity in pre-delivery and delivery — standing, and off three strides and five strides. — Simulation drills, as above, using varied implements. — Practice short, elastic, final stride. — Jumping and conditioning to develop the legs, including two-handed weight throwing.
NOSE DOWN Short flight Rotates forwards	— Incorrect approach rhythm. — Poor placement of hand/javelin/forearm. — The lift in the final action is more dominant than horizontal thrust.	— Improve the rhythm of the approach run. — Correct the relative positioning and action of the shoulder and all upper extremities. — Adjust the timing of the rear leg strike. — Simulation drills single-handed from standing, and from assorted approaches, making the line of pull along the intended line of flight.

JAVELIN FLIGHT FAULTS, CAUSES AND CORRECTIONS

FAULTS	COMMON CAUSES	CORRECTIONS
MISALIGNED TO RIGHT Lands pointing to right Goes out to right	— Misalignment of the javelin to the right during withdrawal. — Leaning too far away to the left at delivery. — Left arm too active in delivery. — Front foot "in the bucket" as the result of a bad cross-step. — Chest comes front-on too soon, because the thrower cannot tolerate the "wound-up" position of the cross-step. — Weak rear-leg activity at delivery because of bad cross-step. — "Breaking" at the waist.	— Practice keeping the javelin tip close to the ear after withdrawal. — Practice keeping the hips to the front during the cross-step. — Repeated drilling of approach, withdrawal and cross-step. — Simulation drills placing the rear foot on the line of run in delivery position. — Practicing the maintenance of straight line forward momentum.
MISALIGNED TO LEFT Lands pointing to left Goes out to left	— Misalignment of the javelin to the left during withdrawal. — Throwing shoulder taken too far round to the rear. — Letting the left side go "soft" during delivery.	— Repeated running with the javelin. — Simulation drills (preferably in front of a mirror) practicing smooth withdrawal begun by the left shoulder. — Simulation drills to improve the left side brace. — Easy throws working at above points — standing, off three or five strides, and 3/4 approach.
VIBRATES EXCESSIVELY	— Incorrect rhythm through the cross-step. — Hesitation between cross-step and delivery. — Body "breaks" and/or wrist relaxes. — Pulling across the javelin's long axis.	— Lengthen the approach run. — Simulation drills working at tightening the wrist, and letting the front foot yield. — Practice smooth transition from approach to delivery. — Start the delivery with the legs to attain the "bow" position before the arm comes into play. — Easy throwing working on above points using stones, light slingballs, from three-stride approach.
INEFFECTIVE RIGHT LEG ACTION	— Weak right leg action. — Simulation drills poorly executed. — Cross-step too high. — Right foot lands passively. — Lack of anticipatory rotation from the pelvis before left foot placement.	— Repeated practice of withdrawal through to transition. — Simulation drills involving rotation of pelvis, linked with outward rotation of the left foot. — Simulation drills involving turning the right knee inward, or the right heel out.

Prepared by V. Mazzilitis, USSR. Translated by Kevin McGill.

TEACHING PROGRESSION FOR THE JAVELIN

The javelin can be taught using a variety of methods. If there is time to approach this without the first competition shortly to follow, which is typical in high school, then the coach may select as many medicine ball drills, weightlifting exercises and specific flexibility exercises as time allows to supplement the basic course of instruction.

The major problem is to teach the use of the legs and hips in the throw. Some coaches have pointed out that the javelin is declining because of a lack of "arms" in the sport. That may also be true; the athlete must establish a correct arm action, surely, but then concentrate on the source of power—the lower body.

You can learn the basics with a variety of implements, if actual throwing with a javelin is impossible at the start. Small medicine balls, weighted balls, nockenballs, and the like, can be used. A few years ago, "stubbies" or short weighted javelins, were available commercially. These could be thrown into a net.

If you have a net, a rubber-tipped javelin might be used indoors. Even if the net resembles a tennis net, you can rig up an old javelin with four "U" shaped clips bolted to the shaft, which would prevent the javelin from passing through.

Step One: The athlete must select a grip that feels comfortable. While the best grip might be the Finnish grip, the very young athlete may be better off with the American grip. Later on, a switch can be made. Make sure that the athlete holds the javelin as if it were an egg—no tightness in the hand. The shaft should rest across the palm, not just up in the fingers as in dart throwing.

Step Two: Have the athlete withdraw the javelin until the tail is higher than the head, and the tip is below eye level. "Flick" the javelin into the ground about 10-15 feet in front. Throwing into a small hillside will do also—less walking, more throws. At this point, we don't mention any corrections, unless it deals with arm action.

Make sure the elbow leads, and then the hand overtakes it in a whip action. If the elbow stays forward, the athlete will toss the javelin like a dart throw, which is typical of young high school athletes.

At release, the hand is high, elbow well above the shoulder. Also, notice the position of the hand after the javelin is gone. Check for the thumb down. This rotation at the shoulder sometimes does not occur because it is not a totally natural reaction. Thumb down, palm out, armpit—this is what the coach should see!

Step Three: Step Two will take a while with some new throwers. Be patient. Step Three is also critical to future success.

First, get the javelin level and instruct the athlete that he/she is to keep the arm as passive as possible. With the athlete in a throwing position, the coach may hold the tail of the implement and go through this slowly at first. Left arm up, weight on the ball of the right foot, left foot on the ground. Have the athlete move the left arm back while turning the right foot, knee, and hip. During this rotation, steer the javelin forward and up.

Inevitably, you may have to stop and work on that tight shoulder! The athlete is working into the "C" position, and the arm delay is absolutely necessary. Make the correction, proceed again.

"Left arm, right leg—together. Relax your arm, forget your arm." Now, the strain on the various joints means that you should go slow, rest, repeat, and so on. With a small group, the coach may have taken 90 minutes up to this point.

Step Four: Each day before practice, the athlete should take a flexible rubber cord and practice Step Three. In addition to being a good technical exercise, Step Three is essential for promoting flexibility prior to the workout. So, make sure we have a warmed-up athlete.

Start with the exact position in Step Three—except the coach will not hold the javelin tail. Have the athlete attempt a short "hip" throw with the left foot on the ground. We tell the athlete to ignore the arm and work the hip.

Of course, we want to correct the arm action, but it is important to teach the leg/hip action first. Watch the right foot and make sure you get a full rotation on the ball of the foot. The right foot has been pointed to about 45 degrees. At completion, the foot should point past zero degrees, or the throwing direction.

Trine Hattestad, 1993 and 1997 World Champion.

The second stage of this step is to have the athlete take a standing throw, with the left foot slightly off the ground at the start. Figure 8 below shows this action. Note the arm delay in this athlete. See how the right foot, knee and hip have come around first.

Figure 8: The Standing Throw.

American record holder Tom Pukstys.

Step Five: This step involves a more technical standing throw. As the athlete learns the previous step, mistakes will be made. This phase may take a few months to master, so this is a continuous learning process.

As the athlete learns to raise the javelin into the proper throwing trajectory, we must pay some attention to the flight of the implement. With easy throws you should get some flat landings. Javelins are rated for distance, and even with the newer javelins, easy flicks from a stand should not force a point-first landing every time.

By "learning to throw flat throws," the athlete is learning to "hit the point." Perhaps those three words sum up the whole event! It is true, you either "hit the point," or you don't. When you don't, you lose a ton of distance. Juris Terauds, in his book, *Biomechanics of the Javelin Throw* (p. 139), talks about finesse, and here is where it comes in. The natural athlete can pick this up in months, but many take years.

Study the flight. Javelin off the palm, point lost, pulling down—we will see these problems regularly at the beginning. Some throwers have remarked that when you hit the point, or pull through the point, you see little of the javelin as it flies away—a silver dollar in the sky.

New rules javelin throwers have to learn proper flighting techniques, as the float factor has been reduced. Leave the thrower alone at times, so he can feel or grasp these things for himself.

Step Six: Step and throw. Figure 9 shows the athlete assuming a different starting position, with the left leg back. You can feel a bit of sinking on the right leg in this drill. And in this exercise we can turn our attention to the plant of the left leg more effectively.

Remember that in the actual throw, we would not want the left leg back like this at the right foot landing. There is right leg action just prior to plant. As long as the force is directed forward, the left leg will land in the proper place. Too large a spread between the legs could mean a late left leg, which may be driven to the left of the proper landing place.

Figure 9: Step and Throw.

Step Seven: Left-right-left. That is also the rhythm you will see in the beginning. Later on, "left—right-left": quick right-left placement.

In Figure 10 below, notice that the athlete has driven himself forward with the left leg. This is an active step which starts with the foot slightly off the ground. It is a step, then drive.

The result is a position in the fifth frame where the athlete is canted rearward on a flexed, powerful right leg, ready to drive the body into that left leg plant. Scissor-step technicians can also practice bringing the right leg back here, for a more active plant.

115

Figure 10: Left—Right-Left.

The athlete in these illustrations uses a passive right leg, but he has a very good left leg action—thus the positions we see.

Notice how in each case, the athlete finishes high with full extension of the left leg. The right arm is last, and the action is near-perfect.

Step Eight: Right-left—right-left. This is almost the same action as the prior step, because the right leg starts on the ground. The only change is that we start with the left leg back. In swinging the left forward, we drive hard with the right to initiate the actual steps. In the actual throw, we would be exactly at the stage after withdrawal of the javelin.

Some coaches skip this step. It may be possible to get right into the javelin approach at this point.

Figure 11 shows what we are attempting to do here. This is a Soviet sequence, typical of the standard approach to learning the field events used in the USSR.

Figure 11: Right-Left—Right-Left.

Step Nine: Now, we will learn the full rhythm of the throw. All steps to this point have had the javelin withdrawn already. With the javelin held level, above eye plane, body facing the throwing direction, and the upper arm perpendicular to the ground, have the athlete keep the javelin in the same place spatially, while walking forward starting with the right leg, and turning shoulders to the side. The coach may hold the javelin tail for this drill.

The left arm will naturally swing forward, as in regular walking or running. With the javelin withdrawn, have the athlete practice walking in this strange posture! Feet ahead, control the javelin—walk, walk, walk. Stop. Repeat until the action is smooth.

Next, have the athlete walk a few steps forward until the left foot lands near a pre-arranged mark.

116

Withdraw, walk, walk. Repeat. Next, have the athlete shuffle-step into a jog, hit the mark, withdraw, jog, jog.

Young athletes might have a flexibility problem here, since the shoulders are sideways and the hips are to the front at this point.

The point of the javelin, for the beginner, should be up slightly at the withdrawal mark. More complex business comes later; we are just at the beginning now. Palm up, javelin straight pullback. It is less a pullback, than it is a walk-away, at first.

The final stage in Step Nine is to incorporate the rhythm of the throw. At the first mark on the left, withdraw, then it is right—left—right—left.

After this is mastered, you work on the second left foot placement. There is a drive here into the throwing stride which resembles a jump, or low hop. The biomechanists point out certain general trends, which start to come into play with the young javelinist. At a clinic in Cologne, Germany, Norwegian authority Edward Harnes listed the following:

- The average stride length should be about 95-98% of the body height.
- L_3 is the second shortest stride of the last four strides.
- L_2 is shorter than L_1.
- L_1 is the longest stride.
- L_0 is the shortest stride.

L_1 is the impulse stride, which means the drive off the left leg has to propel the body horizontally 10-15% longer than the average stride length. The throwing stride, or L_0, is the shortest stride, that is the right leg we are striving to hit as quickly as possible.

We mention this here for the coach, as a reminder that these final strides are what makes the throw.

It is not possible or important to detail every subtle move from every thrower. The study by Harnes of several world class female performers shows the level at which elite coaches study the event. For the athlete, the coach simplifies the details: "It's like a left—right—left, then a jump off the left onto a quick RIGHT-LEFT."

The ratio of L_1 to L_0 is 1.62 to 1.00 in the top throwers. That means that if your athlete had a 7-foot impulse step, the actual distance between the feet in the throwing stride would only be 4'3$\frac{1}{2}$". You don't learn this by marking the field and hitting exact inches, but by many, many hours or practice.

Step Ten: The athlete must work on the whole throw, incorporating a runup. Start with a few strides and work up to eight or ten. Fewer for the beginner, more for the experienced athlete. When Tommi Viskari, the 1990 World Junior Champion from Finland, competed at Amsterdam High School, N.Y., it was shocking to see his quick sprint into the throw. In recent years, American throwers seem to have slowed down, although lately that's been changing.

The advanced technician in the 90s will learn to throw off a fast run and fast steps in the throwing strides.

Repeated practice in the runup will pay big dividends. It will help to avoid fouling, and you'll be working on the throw, instead of watching the foul line. Figure 12 will again show the complete runup.

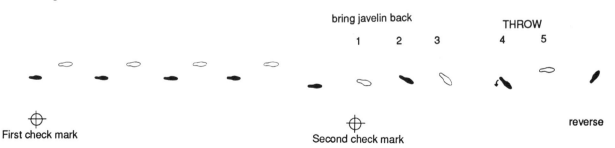

Figure 12: The Complete Runup.

117

JAVELIN DRILLS

The javelin lends itself to all sorts of exercises. Tom Petranoff's javelin video offers a few we cannot recommend: standing on the roof of a house and tossing a medicine ball back and forth to your friend on the ground, for starters. Otherwise, the Petranoff video does show many of the following drills quite well. Dr. Robert Sing's book on the javelin, the event's bible, also shows many drills and is essential reading.

Drill #1. Flexibility with the javelin. There are dozens of possibilities here for the thrower: shown below is only a small sample.

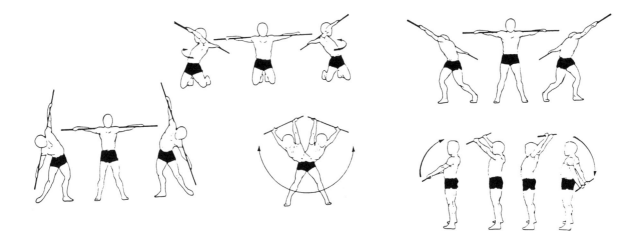

Drill #2. Flexibility with a partner. You can do stretches on your own, but the javelin demands more: learn some partner stretches and you will increase your flexibility.

Drill #3. Throwing stubbies. These were invented by American coach Ed Tucker and came in three weights. Stubbies are short javelins, with crutch tips on the ends, and are perfect for tossing into a net when it is too cold to work out outside. There was a plastic grip on the shaft which approximated the javelin grip. Unfortunately, stubbies are impossible to find now, but they can surely be made in a metal shop. The weight was somewhat balanced at both ends. All that is necessary would be tubing, short pieces of bar stock, and some crutch tips.

From Doherty's *Track & Field Omnibook*, 1985.

Drill #4. Throws with a hollow pipe going up a piece of cable. West Point had one of these in the 1960's. If you have an indoor arena, these can be easily installed. You can experiment with the angle and the weights.

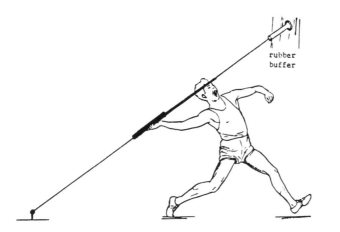

rubber buffer

From Doherty's *Track & Field Omnibook*, 1985.

Drill #5. Finnish medicine ball drills. See Medicine Ball Training in the "Training For Throwers" chapter. There are 46 exercises depicted. This selection was adapted from an article by Lauri Immomen, "Training for Javelin Throw in Finland," which appeared in *Track and Field Quarterly Review*, Vol. 78, #1, pp. 32-38.

In the past few years many different medicine balls have appeared. Banish to the boxing gym the old leather models. The new rubber balls are superior and will last for years, with reasonable use. They are imported and a bit pricey, however. (A set of five in 1990, 1kg-5kg, cost in the neighborhood of $385.)

Recently, some companies have offered the "equipped ball," which is a medicine ball with a hole in it. This permits more exercises of a plyometric nature, since the ball can easily be suspended from an overhead support.

Drill #6. General circuit training, from Soviet coach L. Matveyev. This is a sample of early season training which can be done to whip javelin throwers into shape. There are hundreds of variations on this theme.

An Example of the General Preparatory Set of Circuit Training.

1. Jumping rhythmically over a low obstacle by pushing off with both feet.
2. Transfering in a tempo from lying into sitting "high angle" position and back again.
3. Pullups in a mixed hang.
4. Transfering from a mixed hang with one's back to the wall bars by bending into a bending hang and back again.
5. Jumping up in a tempo from a lying support by pushing off with both feet into a hanging position.
6. Transfering from a hang into a "high angle" hang on the wall bars.
7. Jump mount into support on the horizontal bars—press up—jump off, etc. in a tempo.
8. Pressing up the bar (20% of the maximum weight) in a tempo while jumping feet apart-feet together.
9. 3 x 15 m sprints.
10. Squats with the bar (75% of the maximum weight).

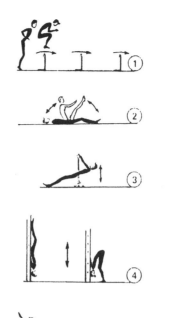
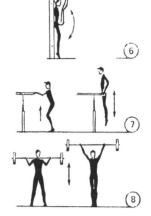

Natalya Shikolenko, 1992 Olympic silver medalist and 1995 World Champion.

Drill #7. Using an axe. This drawing, adapted from an old Russian text, shows the athlete pounding an axe into a pole. We hope the pole is not a living tree, as it appears to be in the Tom Petranoff video! Robert Sing's book has an excellent variation: suspend a log horizontally with sturdy chains overhead—at just enough height to catch the head of a swinging sledge hammer. Wear goggles for your eyes, please! A wood chip can do lots of damage. Coach Bill Webb uses yet another variation with the log placed in the side of a hill, where the athlete can kneel down and pound away. All of these exercises build tremendous strength in the muscles used in the javelin, but have to be done with care.

Drill #8. Hip drills with rubber cables. You can either buy surgical tubing from any hospital supply place or buy a "javee." The javee is a device which comes in two sizes, has three elastic cords attached, with a javelin grip on a short piece of aluminum tubing. Both devices do the same thing.

It is not wise to actually pull the cable with your arm. Why? this will develop some bad habits in the actual throw.

The main use of rubber-cable devices is to stretch your shoulder while you practice some rotation of the rear leg. Tom Petranoff showed me a way to use the left arm in a separate drill. Throw the cable over a goal post or some kind of overhead support. Practice blocking the left side as you pull back on the cable with the left arm.

Drill #9. Thows with a nockenball. The nockenball is a very helpful tool, since you can actually teach youngsters the correct javelin arm action with the ball. We are concerned in the beginning about sidearm tosses. When you throw the nockenball, the little nub rotates and tells you actually how well you have released the ball. These are widely available in several track equipment catalogs. Rubber balls with weights in them are also available, but these can be easily made by stuffing a tennis ball with lead weights and taping it up. Rubber batons for throwing are available, too.

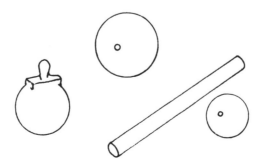

Drill # 10. Throws with normal, light, and heavy javelins. Table 1 is from the IAAF magazine, *New Studies in Athletics,* and shows the East German approach. Table 2 shows the Finnish approach, as presented by Esa Utriainen at the 1987 Aix-Les-Bains Congress. The pronounced difference in total throws seems remarkable but that is explained in that the Finnish totals included ALL throws, even with throwing balls, etc., and the East Germans only counted javelin throws. The Finnish throws are 30-50% with the javelin, so we can say that the totals are comparable.

What weights do you use? Finnish women usually throw 400-600-gram weights, and the men 400-700 for underweight throwing. For heavy throwing, the women usually use 700-900, rarely 1000 grams. The men usually go up to 1500 grams.

The problem in the USA is simple, yet complex. How do we develop young throwers if they are restricted by high school rules as to practice time during the year? With so few states competing in the javelin at the prep level, we are just not getting a sufficient number of 18-year-old throwers. How can young American throwers at age-16 achieve German or Finnish totals in throwing? Presently, they cannot. Most of our best high school throwers start training only in springtime. Meanwhile, their Finnish counterparts are in year-long training programs. Something will have to change for the USA to be competitive.

Table 1

Number of specific throws per year and required performance values							
Implement	Men				Women		
Value in kg.	16y.	17y.	18y.	19y.	16y.	17y.	18y.
Competitive javelin	2,700	3,200	3,500	4,000	2,800	3,300	3,700
Light javelin	600	600	500	500	400	300	400
Heavy javelin	—	—	700	1,000	—	50	800
Competitive javelin	64.00	68.00	74.00	78.00	50.00	55.00	60.00
Light javelin	69.00	73.00	79.00	83.00	55.00	60.00	65.00
Heavy javelin	—	—	60.00	65.00	—	48.00	53.00

From *New Studies in Athletics*, Vol. 3, No. 1, p. 72.

Table 2

	WOMEN		MEN	
	16yrs	22yrs	16yrs	22yrs
Javelin	3,000	5,000	2,000	5,000
Underweight	3,000	4,000	1,000	3,000
Overweight	700-800	1,500	3,000	4,000
Totally	**6,800**	**10,500**	**6,000**	**11,000**

From *The Throws*, European Athletics Coaching Assn. Congress, 1987.

Drill #11. Weightlifting for the javelin. The list of possible exercises could fill this book. Below is a list of exercises done in Finland, as well as in the most important American javelin centers. The major exercises are usually cycled, which means that the athlete can obtain a specific workout geared to the season. Assistance exercises are done only when specified. One would not do all of these at once or you would not have time for throwing! Brief comments follow some of the more unusual exercises:

Major lifts for the javelin:

1. Power snatch
2. Power clean
3. Jerk
4. Front squat
5. Back squat

6. Chair squat—touch chair briefly with buttocks, push up with legs and rise up on toes.
7. Bench press

Assistance exercises:

1. Snatch grip high pulls
2. Sideways lunge—bar on back, spread legs wide, lower one leg, go down, keeping back straight, repeat other side.
3. Half squat jump
4. Good morning
5. Inclined leg lifts on board

Power assistance exercises:

1. Hold a plate in the throwing hand, palm up, while in power position.
2. Javelin isometrics. Hold front of javelin with free hand and push back, while you try and pull forward.
3. Bent arm pullover
4. Seated twist with barbell
5. Standing twist with barbell
6. French press
7. Walking twist with plate held in front
8. Leg twists from a hang
9. Reverse deadlift from a bench, light weight. Grab bar behind your back, while it rests on a bench. Slowly stand up, keeping arms straight.

There are many other exercises that you can do. Curls have little place in this kind of training routine. Big arms do not make javelins fly.

Drill #12. Hose drags while doing cross-steps. You can either drag a hose, a plate, or a frisbee with a weight in it. Current Washington State javelin thrower Chad McKinney did this last variation while in high school.

Drill #13. Carioca with the javelin. This is an excellent drill which gets the athlete in shape, as well as makes for better flexibility.

Drill #14. One-step, two-step, or three-step throws. These are from the teaching progression and are preferred to standing throws. You can work the block from this drill, while you cannot really work the block from a stand.

JAVELIN TRAINING

Javelin training has become fairly sophisticated. Norwegian Coach Ed Harnes has even created a computer program called "Assistant Coach" which can devise workout samples for the coach who is unfamiliar with or resists periodization. There are a number of other coach/programmers at work on the subject of organizing training, and, before long, there will be a few more choices for the coach to organize training by computer.

As with other throwing events, when one talks about organizing a training plan, the debt owed to Soviet coach Anatoliy Bondarchuk is enormous. As the most successful hammer coach ever, Bondarchuk has continuously impressed the throwing world, particularly since the 21-year-old Yuriy Syedikh won the Olympics in 1976. In his many clinics throuhout the world, Bondarchuk has graciously outlined his programs for coaches to understand.

In the javelin, Finns have taken the work of the periodization specialists to the top level. Take a look at all the drills and ideas in the drill section. How does one put all these parts together? First, use common sense; second, don't be afraid to experiment.

Anders Borgstrom, a Swedish coach, has stated that prior to the advent of the new javelin, the Swedes figured that you have to be big and strong to throw far. So they lifted very heavily. They learned, however, that the new javelin demands even more precision than the old. The lesson was learned: technique comes first!

From *New Studies in Athletics* (Vol. 3, No. 1, p. 73), the IAAF journal, we can study the following chart from the East German coaches:

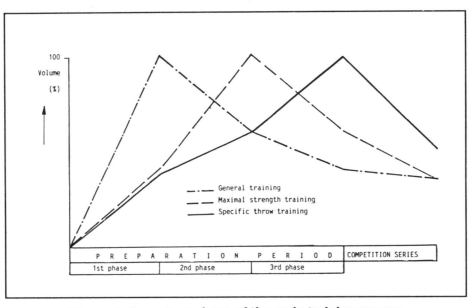

Figure 1: Accentuated use of the main training means.

The coaches have drawn three simple lines which describe the volume of general training, maximal strength training, and specific throw training. You can see how each aspect peaks prior to the beginning of the competition season.

Javelin throwers have to be aware that this is an annual plan and is difficult to transcribe to the March 15th-June 1st thrower.

This is one way of looking at the annual plan. The note in the article states that this model has been practiced in the GDR for more than 20 years.

It is necessary to note that each year the total volume for the thrower in the German model is increased 10-15%. This means that there are long range multi-year plans in effect, and their results are sufficient to prove that this system is effective.

How they create these numbers in the javelin is shown next. Of course, these are guidelines, and there is up to a 400-throw leeway.

Figure 2: East German volume guides and required strength performances.

Volume guiding values (yearly sums) and required performances in the strength training of adolescent javelin throwers				
Age group	Volume	Snatch	Required performance Bench pressing	Squat
16 male	2,400-2,600	75.00 kg.	80.00 kg.	140.00 kg.
17 male	2,800-3.200	80.00	85.00	150.00
18 male	3,400-3,800	92.50	90.00	160.00
19 male	4,000-4,200	105.00	95.00	170.00
16 female	2,400-2,600	50.00	55.00	110.00
17 female	2,800-3,200	55.00	65.00	120.00
18 female	3,400-3,800	65.00	70.00	130.00

From *New Studies in Athletics*, Vol. 3, No. 1, p. 71.

This is a disciplined approach, which worked time and again for the German throwers. Recent political developments (German reunification) may greatly affect this kind of plan being carried out in the future.

The Finns have a similar approach to the javelin—very disciplined in the annual plans. Coach Esa Utriainen, in his book on the javelin, has described some of the microcycles or weekly charts for volume and intensity. We will look at one for a general period and two examples of the competition period for comparison.

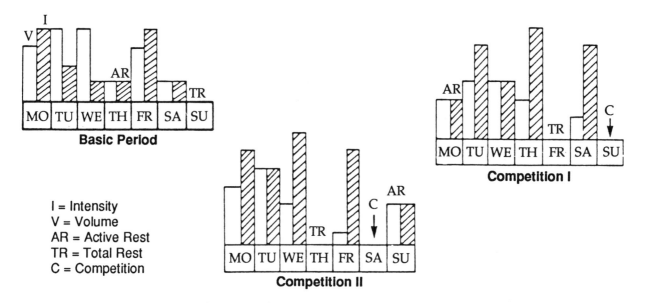

I = Intensity
V = Volume
AR = Active Rest
TR = Total Rest
C = Competition

A few generalizations can be made: 1) the volume is greatly decreased in the competition period. If you were taking 50 throws earlier, this volume would be down to 35 or so, maximum, and even less on some days; 2) the *intensity* of the work is much higher in the competition period. The thrower should not exhaust himself with 100 throws, but he should take some hard throws, close to competition effort. General training for Bondarchuk is approximately 80% of maximum distance. Competition training sometimes can surpass the maximum in the meet (!); 3) notice the variety in the approach. These athletes are not bored with the same old thing. The coaches are mixing up the training.

This concludes our brief look at javelin training. By plugging in all the parts discussed in the drills, you can become an artist. While there is science behind the approach, javelin throwing cannot be learned from a book. Just as you can't name too many famous artists who took lessons at the local "Y" and then quickly found fame and fortune, so it is with coaching and throwing. You experiment, practice and work hard and find out what works in your situation. Good luck!

TEST FOR JAVELIN THROWERS

Refer to the training chapter for a description of the Max Jones test. As a supplement to that test, we will outline a Finnish test used which is included in Esa Utriainen's book *Javelin Throw,* a 292-page masterpiece on the javelin.

The Test Quadrathlon has one advantage over the Finnish test—the scoring tables. What the javelin coach must do is keep careful records for this test and use them over the years for comparative analysis. With 20 items in the test, the coach will have a wealth of data for future training years. While the distance of the throw itself is the final test, the coach is always searching for a way to make the big throws come more often.

One advantage in this test is the section on flexibility. The javelin demands a great deal of flexibility in the arm and shoulder in order to delay the arm in the delivery. A tight shoulder will make this impossible.

Young throwers may want to develop flexibility too quickly and this is a danger the coach must watch out for. Most youngsters must build up slowly in performing shoulder dislocates, and the like, as the potential for harm is always there.

With younger throwers, you may want to have the weightlifting recorded in sets of five or more, to avoid the dreaded one-rep maximum syndrome.

Coach Utriainen offers the following list of suggestions for running the tests: 1) do not do this all on the same day; 2) do not test too many athletes at once, and have a delay in-between sets; 3) repeat tests under exactly the same conditions each time.

If enough coaches use this test, perhaps we can gather the results and prepare norms for our throwers. One difference between the USA and the other countries is the lack of standardization in matters such as this. That is what we get for being such a large country.

TEST:	RECORDS:	11	12	1	2	3	4	5	6	7	8
30m sprint	_____										
20m fly run	_____										
12-min. run	_____										
Standing long jump	_____										
3 jumps	_____										
5 jumps	_____										
Backwards shot throw (kg)	_____										
Forward shot throw (kg)	_____										
Overhead forward throw (kg)	_____										
Clean	_____										
Snatch	_____										
Parallel squat	_____										

THROW

Underweight (kg)	_____										
Underweight (kg)	_____										
Overweight (kg)	_____										
Overweight (kg)	_____										

MOBILITY REPORT:

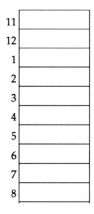

Forward body bend - measure from top of fingertips.

11	
12	
1	
2	
3	
4	
5	
6	
7	
8	

Trunk backbend - measure fingertips to heel. Keep heel on floor.

11	
12	
1	
2	
3	
4	
5	
6	
7	
8	

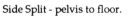

Side Split - pelvis to floor.

11	
12	
1	
2	
3	
4	
5	
6	
7	
8	

Shoulder flexibility - measure minimum grip width. Keep arms straight.

11	
12	
1	
2	
3	
4	
5	
6	
7	
8	

TEST FOR JAVELIN THROWERS From Esa Utriainen

JAVELIN THROW REFERENCES AND SUGGESTED READING

1. Arbeit, E. et. al., 1988. "The Javelin: The View Of The DVfL Of The GDR. *New Studies in Athletics.* Vol. 3, #1, pp. 57-74.

2. Brown, Harmon. "Javelin Throwing, British Style." *Track Technique.* No. 120. Summer 1992.

3. Doherty, Ken. *Track & Field Omnibook.* 4th edition. Los Altos: Tafnews Press, 1985.

4. Dyson, Geoffrey. *Dyson's Mechanics of Athletics.* London: Hodder and Stoughton, 1987.

5. Jonath, U., et al. *Leichtathletik 2.* Hamburg: Rowohlt, 1977.

6. Khomenkova, L.S. *A Textbook for the Track and Field Coach.* Moscow: USSR Government Publishing Office, 1982.

7. Kruber, Dieter and Arnulf. *Der Speerwurf.* Berlin: Verlag Bartels and Wernitz KG, 1972.

8. Matveyev, L. *Fundamentals of Sports Training.* Moscow: Progress Publishing, Inc., 1981.

9. Mazzilitis, V. *Skepa Mesana.* Riga, 1963.

10. McGill, Kevin. "In Search of Seppo." *Track Technique.* No. 126. Winter 1994.

11. Payne, Howard, ed. *Athletes In Action.* London: Pelham Books, 1985.

12. Sing, Robert. *The Dynamics of the Javelin Throw.* Cherry Hill: Reynolds Publishing, Inc., 1984.

13. Terauds, Juris. *Biomechanics of the Javelin Throw.* Del Mar: Academic Publishers, 1985.

14. Utriainen, Esa. "Difference in Men's and Women's Training for Javelin," *The Throws,* Paris: AEFA, 1987.

15. Utriainen, Esa. *Keihaanheitto.* Helsinki: Suomen Urheilulitto, 1987.

AERODYNAMICS AND MECHANICS

DISCUS

The discus and the javelin are the two throwing events where aerodynamics plays a large part. The science of the discus was advanced in large measure by the work of Dick Ganslen in the 1950s. Let's look at some illustrations by Howard Payne (from *The Science of Track and field Athletics*) which show the basics of discus aerodynamics:

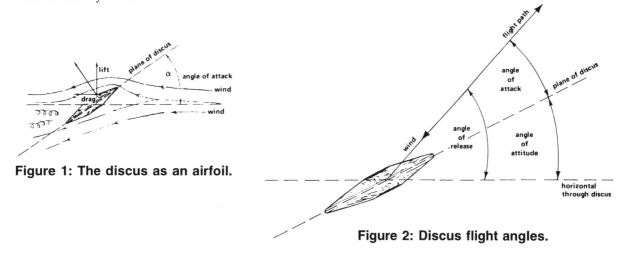

Figure 1: The discus as an airfoil.

Figure 2: Discus flight angles.

In Figure 1, the discus is described by Payne as an airfoil. The effect of the forces of the air on the discus can be broken into two components: lift (vertical) and drag (horizontal). The angle of attack can be thought of as just that—the angle at which the discus is "attacking" the wind in relation to the discus.

An athlete who does not release the discus with the thumb in control will usually let the front edge go way up. You've seen what happens—the discus falls like it was shot out of the sky. Imagine the discus in the illustration tilted up more towards the vertical. Not a very good idea.

Figure 2 clearly shows the attack angle. In the Montreal Olympics, Mac Wilkins's winning throw had a -19.0-degree angle of attack, similar to what is shown in the second drawing. This kind of angle is necessary for stability of the discus in flight because of wind factors and effects of the rotating discus.

All the coach must know about this is: work on a negative attack angle by practicing the release of the discus. It is difficult to measure this exactly without expensive equipment. The other consideration is release angle—in top throwers it is approximately 34-39 degrees.

To take into account the characteristics of flight, equipment makers have designed several discuses for throwers of different ability. One manufacturer produces four types: a) much of the weight in the middle; b) 70% of the weight on the rim; c) 80% on the rim; d) 90% on the rim.

A beginning thrower who throws with the (d) model will achieve nothing but a discus wobbling like crazy. That discus is strictly for national-class throwers; it would be a waste of money for the young thrower to buy one. Beginners should start with the (a) model or an equivalent and work up the line.

WIND AND DISCUS

Kim Bukhantsev, USSR, was reported by Bogdan Poprawski in the April 1989 *Athletics* (Canada) to have made a number of interesting comments on what to do in the wind. The summary is as follows:

Headwind. Lower release angle to 27 degrees and the angle of attack to -4 degrees when you are throwing into a 10mps wind. If you throw with an angle of attack of +4 degrees, you will lose 4.5 meters on the throw!

Right side wind. This is ideal for the right-handed thrower. The angle of release should be up to 32 degrees, and the direction of the throw should be toward the right sector line. The right edge of the discus should be either parallel with the left, or slightly lower.

Left side wind. This is usually a disaster for righties. With a 10mps wind, keep the release angle the same as the right side, 32 degrees. Throw down the left sector with the right edge lower than the left.

Tailwind. This reduces air resistance, so the throw suffers. Increase the angle of release to approximately 43 degrees at 8mps wind, and to the amazing military angle of 45 degrees if the wind reaches 10mps.

Calm. Mac Wilkins threw in calm conditions in the 1976 Olympics. The Russian coach advises an angle of release of 36-40 degrees like Wilkins. A negative angle of attack up to -14 degrees is advised. We have noted already that Wilkins had a -19.0 degrees on his Olympic winning toss. A 53.80m toss with those recommendations will be reduced 1.17m by just using a zero-degree angle of attack, all conditions equal.

Comment: The material above may be more interesting to the elite competitor, but younger throwers should motivate themselves to work hard on technique so that if a change has to be made to win a competition, the adjustment can be made.

It is tough to do this under the pressure of a meet. Be sure to practice in all conditions so that you can experience for yourself what the wind direction can do to a discus. Reading this is not a substitute for throwing practice.

JAVELIN

Juris Terauds is the acknowledged master of javelin aerodynamics. We will start with his drawing on the terminology used in this subject:

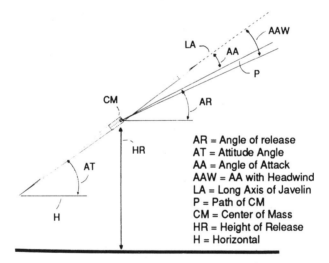

AR = Angle of release
AT = Attitude Angle
AA = Angle of Attack
AAW = AA with Headwind
LA = Long Axis of Javelin
P = Path of CM
CM = Center of Mass
HR = Height of Release
H = Horizontal

TERMINOLOGY FOR JAVELIN RELATED ANGLES.
Note that in the case of a headwind the angle of attack is larger than it would be in still air.
In the same fashion a tailwind diminishes the angle of attack.

From Juris Terauds, *Biomechanics of the Javelin Throw*, 1985.

Glossary of terms:

• Angle of Release—acute angle between the horizontal and the path of the javelin's center of mass.
• Attitude Angle—this is the angle between the long axis of the javelin and the horizontal.
• Angle of Attack—this is the acute angle between the long axis of the javelin and its direction in the air (path of javelin's center of mass).
• Long Axis of Javelin—this is the exact center of the javelin along its length.
• Path of CM—this is the direction in which the center of mass of the javelin is traveling.
• CM—this is the center of mass in the javelin. It is shown to be near the front of the grip.
• Height of Release—this is the measurement from the ground to your hand at the moment of release.
• Horizontal—You know what that is!

There is one problem here. The javelin is so affected by the wind that certain angles will change in flight. There is a pitching moment, which varies according to the release velocity, the effect of wind, and the implement used. Terauds has written that the lower the thrower can throw, the more velocity he is able to reach but there is a point where this will not help.

All of this is fine, but what happens if you make one simple error such as pulling down on the shaft? It is all over. You must simply attempt to have a clean release, with as little vibration in the shaft as possible.

In still air, the ideal angle of attack should be zero. If you increase the angle of attack too much, you will have a stalling problem, which greatly reduces the flight distance. Terauds stresses throwing *finesse;* the thrower must simply practice until his release is perfect.

It is really impossible to discuss the ideal angle of release, since this will vary from thrower to thrower. There are so many variables which must be taken into account. High school boys are throwing the old javelin most of the time, though we hear of schools where they throw the new javelin! It is hard to generalize with that situation.

Recent research by Swedish coach Anders Borgström presented evidence that the rotations of the javelin at release can definitely increase the flight. He presents the following Javagun experimentation comparisons:

THE NEW JAVELIN

	JAVAGUN *		TOP THROWERS **	
	Without rotations V_0: 27.8 m/sec	With rotations 21.5/sec. V_0: 28.3 m/sec		
OLD	82.18	84.60	86.25	
NEW	78.74	79.58	79.30	80.00
DIFERENCE	4.2%	5.9%	8.1%	7.3%

* Average of 300 shots with the Javagun. Models from NORDIC, HELD AND APOLLO
** Average of athletes ranked 21-50 in the Worldlist from 1985 (old), 1986 (new) and 1987 (new).

COEFFICIENT OF CORRELATION; THROWING DISTANCE AND SPEED OF RELEASE (V_0).

OLD   r. + 0.90 - = 0.97   (Ikegami, Miura, Matsui & Hashimoto/1981; Terauds/1987; Komi & Mero/1985)
NEW   R. + 0.80 - + 0.87   (Borgström & Almström/1986)

From *New Studies in Athletics*, Vol. 3, No. 1, pp. 85-88.

This chart shows that the rotations of 21.5/sec. had a dramatic effect on the throwing distance, as shot from the Javagun. What this means is that the Finnish javelin grip is perhaps the best choice since this grip will enable the thrower to rotate the javelin much more than the fork grip, which some have experimented with.

CONCLUSION

Being sure to follow up and get some of the recommended readings. This brief look at the basics of the throws is meant merely as an introduction to the subject. There is a great deal of material out there for the interested coach to pursue.

The reader should pick up texts by Hay, Ecker, or Dyson on mechanics to go further than the brief discussion in this book. For the javelin, Juris Terauds' text *Biomechanics of the Javelin Throw,* is a must for those wishing to understand the old javelin vs. new javelin mechanics. Recently, the women's javelin has been altered, but there has been no research published yet on its flight characteristics.

TRAINING FOR THROWERS

PLANNING THE TRAINING YEAR (MACROCYCLE)

The above heading can be misleading, since most high school coaches do not have a year to train their athletes. Whether the training "year" is three, six or nine months, the same basic principles are used. In all cases, the training schedule is divided into three parts: the Preparation Phase, the Competition Phase and the Transition Phase. Perhaps more meaningful description of these different phases is the Development Phase, Maintenance Phase and Reduction Phase. A term used to describe the planning of the training schedule is called *Periodization*.

Planning is critical. The coach must be sure that when he trains his athletes, they will be able to reach their maximum athletic potential at the right time.

Planning must consider every aspect of training—nothing must be left out. In the 1972 Munich Olympic Games, the three medal winners in the men's shot put were within three-quarters of an inch of each other. Who can say what aspect of training may have been neglected to shunt a possible gold medal winner to bronze?

To plan the yearly training program properly the coach must list all the components that are necessary for the "complete" development of the athlete to meet the specific needs of the event. Listed below are the basic components and their indices for the throwing events:

- Technique
- Weight Training
  General
  Specific
  Olympic
- Plyometrics
  Jumps
  Specific
- Variable Throws
  General
  Specific
  Speed
  Strength
- Medicine Ball Drills
- Flexibility & Balance
- Running
  Anaerobic
  Aerobic

Once a coach has determined the components of his training program, he must put these components into the "yearly" training plan (periodization). To determine the different phases of the year, the coach has to count backward from the state championship meet (if that's your main goal) to the start of the season when he can begin training the athletes.

If the season is six or nine months, then most likely there will be an indoor season along with an outdoor season. Or, in the southern states, because of the weather, the season could start in January and there could be outdoor meets as early as February. In either case, the coach has to plan what is called a *double periodization* training schedule, in which he has the athletes peak twice during the year.

Usually, the *Competitive or Maintenance Phase* is four to five weeks long. It is during this time that the athlete backs off from a lot of hard volume work and settles into a short intense schedule. On the elite level, there may possibly be three or four Competitive Phases of only two to three weeks. It all depends on how many peaks the athlete is capable of. On the high school level, the coach automatically reduces the volume during the month of May in preparation for the state meet.

There is much debate regarding exactly how and when the athlete should reduce the volume of training before the championship meet. It depends a great deal on the athlete involved. Studies have shown one athlete can reach his peak form in two months, whereas another needs six months. It all depends on the adaptability of the body to the different stresses placed upon it. This is referred to as *individualization of the training plan*.

As the coach gets to know his athlete and his responses to the different training stimuli over the years, he is eventually able to pretty well predict and plan the training so that the athlete peaks at the right time. This takes some years of experience by the coach and record keeping of each athlete's training components in great detail. This record keeping is routine on the elite level. The high school coach does not have the time and the record keeping abilities that the specialist coach has on the elite level.

After the coach has determined the number of months, which are called *mesocycles*, (a mesocycle is usually made up of a four-week block of time—a month), he decides when he will put in the Preparation

Phase(s) and Competitive Phase(s). If the state meet is in May and the coach wants his athlete to peak for this meet, and if the season starts March first, then the Preparation Phase would be during the months of March and April, while the Competitive Phase would be during May. There are three Mesocycles in this particular *Macrocycle*.

Or, if the season starts in January and there is an indoor season, the first Preparation Phase would be during the months of January and February with the first Competitive Phase during the first two or three weeks of March. Then there would be another Preparation Phase during the last one or two weeks of March and the month of April. The final Competitive Phase would be the month of May when the athlete would peak for the state meet. This is an example of a Double Periodization Macrocycle. If the athlete can start training in September or November, the Preparation Phase starts at that time and continues until the first competitive phase.

If the athlete is planning to continue into the summer competitions, such as the Junior Olympics, the coach has to schedule another Preparation Phase of three or four weeks to take the neuromuscular system to a higher level of conditioning.

The Transition Phase is that part of the training year when the athlete goes into *active rest*. Even the three- and six-month track season athletes should consider active rest because most of them were probably involved in other sports or were on a weight training schedule before the official start of the track season. By active rest, we mean that the athlete does not totally shut down, but continues weight training at a much lower intensity and only twice a week. He also gets involved in other sports, such as soccer, basketball, racquetball, swimming, etc., where he will not experience great loss of muscle tonus. The important thing is to take a vacation from any throwing sessions and other stressful training.

If an athlete does not take advantage of this recovery period, he is opening himself up to future injury because of overtraining and the danger of getting stale or losing interest in the sport. It takes an exceptional athlete to be able to maintain a high intensity schedule over a period of years in only one sport without losing the desire to continue.

It is assumed that any dedicated high school thrower will be involved in a strength training program, even though he is involved in other sports. With this assumption, I emphasize the need for the athlete to enter into a four-week cycle of recovery—even on the high school level.

Examples of yearly training cycles for high school:

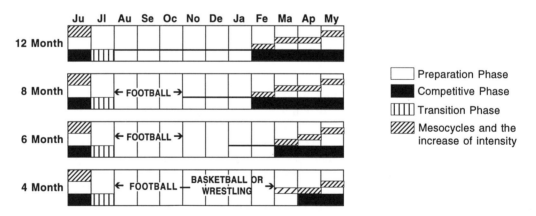

The above schedules are for those athletes who are able to train for twelve months and those who are restricted by state rules or are involved in other sports.

If an athlete is injured or becomes sick or is forced to interrupt his training, he must catch up on his preparation training and should start the competition phase later . . . if he expects to be successful.

MICROCYCLE

Another term that it often used in training is *Microcycle*. A Microcycle is anything from three to seven days. The Microcycle is really the core of the training program. The coach can have the Macrocycles, Phases, and Mesocycles down on paper, but the basic center of the training program is the Microcycle. It involves the day-to-day activities of each training session.

The coach must have a master plan for the year and have a basic outline of where he is taking the athlete

. . . goals! Once the coach has determined the exercises, drills, etc. that he plans to use and has placed them in the approximate times of the Macrocycle, Mesocycle and Phases, he has a better grasp on his ability to develop a Microcycle.

For example, he would use general exercises during the Preparation Phases, then special exercises at the end of the Preparation Phase and the start of the Competition Phase. From there he would introduce the specific exercises of the event(s) during the rest of the Competitive Phase for peaking the athlete.

The development of the Microcycle takes time and should be as individualistic as possible. On the elite level, this involves a program for each individual athlete. On the high school level, the coach is forced to develop "individual" programs for groups of athletes who are at similar basic technical and physical levels. If the coach has a real feel for his athletes, he may be able to individualize certain aspects of their training.

There are many aspects of the training program that can change and alter the whole schedule. For example, the athlete may be injured for a short or long period of time, the family may go on vacation during the usual school breaks, or he may become "overtrained" which forces the coach to completely change the originally planned program. Or it may be that the athlete is even undertrained and the program has to be upgraded and intensified. There is no one definitive prescription to a training program. But, if the coach has some idea of where he is going by having a basic Macrocycle plan with the approximate schedule for his Mesocycles and Phases, then he should easily be able to do his weekly or Microcycle plans.

With the understanding that the Microcycle is the key to training, it is essential that the coach plan the daily sessions of the Microcycle carefully so that every aspect necessary for the complete training of the athlete is included. Nothing must be left to chance. Don't cheat your athlete by not planning his program carefully. Have a checklist of every drill and exercise that will be used during the training program. Making use of the computer is an excellent way of recording every aspect of the athlete's training. The author uses a special program (D & D Software Inc.) in which he is able to record exactly when, how many, and how much any drill and exercise are used during the training year. We use it to develop every Microcycle for each individual thrower in the program.

TECHNIQUE

The first component in our list, technique, is self-explanatory, except to say that today's elite athletes spend as much time on technique refinement as they do on overall conditioning and strength training. All things being equal, the athlete who possesses the most functional technique in terms of biomechanics will be the winner. Usually on the elite level, the strength indices are pretty well developed. It is the fine tuning of the technique that makes the difference between success and failure.

For the novice thrower in high school, it is even more important that technique be given its proper place in the training program, and it must be good technique. Any coach can make an athlete strong, but it takes a *teacher* to make a champion.

Technique can be affected by the lack of strength of the novice athlete, and so there is a time when strength training may require a greater emphasis than technique work. When working with the novice athlete for the first time, light implements should be used. After the athlete has reached a degree of proficiency with a particular weight, then the coach moves him up to a heavier weight. It may be necessary that the athlete use nothing more than a softball for the shot put and a gym shoe for the discus. The technique must not be altered because the novice cannot handle an implement that is too heavy for him.

STRENGTH TRAINING

Strength training is a critical component in events that require strength, explosive power and speed. It is often asked if an athlete can have too much strength. The answer is "yes and no." Yes, if it means he weight trains to the exclusion of the other components, hoping that great strength will overcome uncertain technique and lack of explosive power. There was a time when many good throwers were of that mind set, but they were soon passed by when the "sophisticated" athlete came upon the scene.

If the athlete is able to train all the other components as well as strength, then he cannot develop too much strength. Strength, of course, is essential. The sophisticated athlete has found that he must divide his training between strength training and the development and refinement of technique.

In modern training, individual athletes have been pushing themselves harder and harder, far beyond what was once considered the limits of training. This shows that athletes' bodies are capable of adapting to greater loads and stress. They have come to realize that "limits exist only in the mind."

Recent studies have shown that very young athletes are capable of lifting heavy weights. This research has found that we have underestimated what these young bodies are capable of doing if they are properly supervised and under the guidance of a good strength coach.

Because of this knowledge, the workloads of today are much more intense than they were a few years ago. However, training must be individualized, because all athletes cannot maintain the same workload. The coach must realize that each athlete is different in terms of being able to work with certain loads, intensities, and implements. So he is required to evaluate each athlete when developing the training program, making sure that the athlete is able to recover from heavy training.

Because of the danger of physical breakdown, the coach and athlete must be conscious of a healthful lifestyle that includes plenty of sleep, good nutrition and abstinence from alcohol, nicotine and, even more important today, drugs.

A common mistake is to imitate the training programs of champions. This can be foolhardy and dangerous. The programs that are reproduced in print are only fragments of the total training program. They don't tell how long the athlete had been preparing to reach a particular stage of his training, if he trained with light or heavy loads during the previous phase, how long he had been training (training age), or what his body's possibilities of recovery were after such efforts. There is just too much important information not revealed in such articles.

(Training age is determined by the number of months the athlete has been training seriously. For example, if he has lifted seriously for six months of one year and six months the follow year, then he is considered to have a training age of one year. Every twelve months of training makes a training age year.)

WHAT TYPE OF TRAINING?

The coach must have some knowledge of the type of strength training that is to be used during the different phases and microcycles. Does the athlete need hypertrophy or does he need explosive strength? These questions and others determine exactly what type of training must be prescribed for the athlete.

First, the coach must decide what type of strength training his athletes need in the different phases of the training schedule. Is the training goal basic strength and hypertrophy (muscle mass)? If so, then the coach uses *Submaximal Contraction Methods*. These methods are characterized by a large number of sets of repetitions with loads of 60-80%. The execution of movement is rapid to slow and *ends in complete muscular failure.* Below are examples of these different methods:

1. The load is constant at 80% with 3-5 sets of 8-10 repetitions with a rest of 3-5 minutes.
2. Ladder method where the load is increased with each set: 12 reps at 70%, 10 reps at 80%, 7 reps at 85%, and 5 reps at 90%.
   The rest between each set is 5 minutes.

   In the two methods above, a training partner is needed, since in any one set, the last repetitions end in failure, and a training partner provides light manual assistance to allow completion of the prescribed repetitions.
3. The extensive bodybuilding method uses light loads of 60-70% of 15-20 reps for 2-3 sets. The rest period between sets is 2-3 minutes and is relatively short. This is a very common bodybuilding method.
4. The intensive bodybuilding method uses 3-5 sets of 5-8 repetitions with 85-95% intensity. The rest periods between sets are 3-5 minutes. Both bodybuilding methods are aimed at total overloading, resulting in fatigue of the muscular system.

Different examples of bodybuilding methods are as follows:

a. Forced Reps. At the end of each set, 2 or 3 additional reps are executed with the help of a training partner. There is *help* during the concentric phase. The athlete does the eccentric phase unassisted.
b. Negative Reps. At the end of a set of concentric contractions that end in failure, 2 to 3 eccentric reps are performed. The training partner lifts the bar so that the athlete can perform the

eccentric contractions.

    c.   Supersets. This is performing two sets without any rest between sets. A superset can be done two ways. The first one is where two different exercises are performed on the same muscle group, i.e., leg extensions, followed by squats. The second method is the exercising of opposite muscle groups, i.e., arm curls, followed by bench press or triceps extensions.

    d.   Cheating Repetitions. This is attempting to do more reps after failure using incorrect movements, such as arching the back during the bench press after bouncing the bar off the chest.

    e.   Pre-exhaustion Principle. This is working a muscle group in a similar fashion to that of supersets. The athlete performs an exercise of a specific muscle group followed without rest by an exercise to a compound muscle group. An example is a set of supine flys to exhaust the pectoral muscles followed immediately by the bench press. The specific exercise is a one-joint exercise, while the compound exercise is a two-joint exercise.

The throws coach must be aware that submaximal methods, if used only over a period of several mesocycles, will have a negative effect upon the fast-twitch muscle fibers. It has been found that if slow movements and submaximal use of strength are used for hypertrophy development only, the athlete runs the risk of becoming less explosive over a period of time.

The method used to develop explosive strength and an improvement in neural activation, along with greater strength potential without gaining a lot of muscle mass, is called the *Maximal Contraction Method*. This method emphasizes neural output and should be practiced in a rested state, because each contraction must be executed with maximal effort and as explosively as possible against loads of 90 to 100% or supramaximal loads of 150%.

1.   The Narrow Pyramid Method is 1 set of 3 reps at 90%, 1 set of 1 at 95%, 1 set of 1 at 97%, 1 set of 1 at 100%, and 1 set 1 at 100% plus 2-3 lbs for a new PR. Rest intervals are 3-5 minutes.

2.   The Eccentric Contractions Method is using loads of slightly above 150% of maximum. Two training partners are used to lift the weight after each eccentric contraction. Each contraction should take 5 to 6 seconds to lower the bar. Five repetitions of 3 sets are used with 3-minute rests between sets.

3.   Concentric and Eccentric Contractions during the same set. This requires the use of a special hook that hangs on the bar and is kicked off at the end of the eccentric contraction. The bar is lowered during the eccentric contraction with 100% of the athlete's max for bench and 110% for squats. As soon as the hooks are released the athlete does a concentric contraction of 60-70%. Five sets of 5 or 6 reps are performed with a 3-minute rest. This is for bench press and squats only. Studies have shown that this is one of the most effective ways to gain explosive strength and power.

Another way to use the Concentric/Eccentric method is to do 3 to 5 sets of 6-8 repetitions at 70% to 90%, using the same weight throughout both types of contractions. The bar is almost free falling, then is suddenly decelerated and, in the shortest time possible, re-accelerated upward. This routine is usually done with only the bench press and squats.

The *Static/Dynamic Method* is another way to put the muscles under great stress using the bench press and squat. In the bench, the athlete lowers the bar until the arms are parallel to the floor. It is held there for two or three seconds and then is lifted as quickly as possible. The amount of weight on the bar is 85% to 95% of the max. The legs are parallel in the squat. When doing this routine, there is one set of four to six repetitions.

Another strength training method that involves both submaximal and maximal training is called the *Mixed Method*. This is using the wide pyramid along with the narrow pyramid. The athlete starts with light loads and high repetitions, then works up to a maximal intensity and low repetitions, after which the repetitions are increased and the load reduced, i.e., 7 reps at 80%, 5 reps at 85%, 3 reps at 90%, 2 reps at 95%, 1 rep at 100%, 3 reps at 90% and 7 reps at 80%. Rest intervals are 3-5 minutes between sets.

Understanding the function of submaximal and maximal contractions enables the coach to schedule these two methods in proper sequence. The use of submaximal contractions during the first few months of a macrocycle enables the athlete to hypertrophy the muscles. During the later part of the preparation phase and into the first part of the competition phase, these two methods of contraction are alternated every two microcycles. Then during the middle and latter stages of the competition phase, only maximal contractions are used.

OLYMPIC LIFTING FOR THROWERS

One aspect of training that cannot be omitted for the serious thrower is the use of Olympic lifts. There is no doubt that Olympic lifting develops explosive power and speed. There is some controversy over which of the lifts, the clean or the snatch, is the more important to the thrower. The snatch offers complete extension of the body in one movement, while the clean allows the athlete to use more weight in pulling the bar to the chest position. From there he is able to get great extension when the bar is jerked overhead.

Some modifications should be used when performing the Olympic lifts. The athlete should use the leg split with the power leg back. If the athlete is right-handed, the right leg is back. Biomechanical studies have shown that the athlete should only use exercises that are related to the short paths of the acceleration and deceleration of the body. Therefore, the snatch should be done from the hang and hip position and half- and quarter-squats should be performed rather than parallel squats.

STRENGTH TRAINING PRINCIPLES

Once the season starts, the athlete is not able to put as much time in in the weight room because of the technique aspects of his training. It is therefore necessary for the coach to start the athlete in strength training as soon as possible. If he is not in other sports, he should start in September, but if he is out for football, he should begin as soon as the season is completed. It would be ideal if he could lift during the football season. This would obviously benefit his football playing as well.

Not too many years ago, it was common for throwers to spend hours in the weight room because there were so many exercises to do. Now research has shown that doing fewer exercises with greater intensity is far more beneficial.

The athlete needs to do only three to four exercises in a day. As long as the athlete trains the main muscle groups that are specific to the event, there is no need to do any more. The intensity and the quality of work are most important.

This may sound contradictory to what has just been said, but the *volume* of work has an extremely important role in the improvement of sport performance. Those who understand this requirement of modern training have achieved superior sports performance.

The important question then is what is meant by volume? What are the limits of volume in the course of an athlete's training? Just how much time does an athlete have to train? Time is the limiting factor that affects the volume of training an athlete is able to handle. On the high school level, time is pretty well controlled by the set schedule of classes, and so on. On the elite level, it becomes necessary for athletes to train more than once a day.

High school athletes usually practice six days a week for three to four hours a day. On the elite level, however, the athlete will work out six to seven days a week and approximately five to six hours on multiple practice days.

Practice hours per six day week:
    High School — 18 - 24 hours

Practice hours per seven day week:
    Elite — 26 - 29 hours

Arrangement of "multiple practices":

1.5 - 1.5 - 1.5 - 1.5	(6 hrs.)
1.5 - 1.5 - 2	(5 hrs.)
2 - 3	(5 hrs.)
1.5 - 1.5 - 1.5	(4.5 hrs.)
1 - 1.5 - 2	(4.5 hrs.)

As can be seen, the training age of the athlete determines the amount of volume he can handle in a week. The 18-hour week is for a novice athlete. As his training age goes up, so do the volume and hours. Volume is not only time, but the number of throws, the number of jumps, the number of sprints, the number of med ball throws, the number of reps lifted and the tonnage, etc.

The length of the practice session has a lot to do with the athlete's training age, experience, etc. It's possible that each practice session could be anywhere from two to four hours long, including both throwing and lifting.

If it is possible to train more than once a day, studies have shown that the best schedule for multiple practices is two to three times a day on Monday, Wednesday, and Friday and only once a day on Tuesday, Thursday and Saturday. When doing multiple practices, specificity should be the order of the day. This means that in the morning practice session(s), technique and plyometic types of training take place, because the nervous system is much less prone to be fatigued. In the afternoon, specific weight training and regular strength training are in order.

Once an athlete begins his training program, he must have as few interruptions as possible. This becomes difficult in the USA when students go on Christmas and Easter holidays. And then there is summer vacation when most students are off for three months—away from the weight room facilities and motivation.

Research has shown that with this many interruptions, the continuity of the training program is disturbed and the training effects that were developed during the months when school was in session are lost, especially during the long summer holiday. It becomes imperative for the coach and serious athlete to continue to train during the periods when school is closed in order to continue strength growth and muscle hypertrophy.

It has been learned that if weight training has been discontinued for three weeks, there is a considerable drop in strength. This is why elite athletes cannot afford to be away from weight training for more than a couple of weeks. The same holds true for the lower level athlete. Three weeks is the maximum that a dedicated athlete can take away from his training.

Even in the weekly (microcycle) plan, research has shown that if an exercise is not performed at least twice a week, there is no carry-over effect to the development of strength. The old adage of changing the exercise for variety's sake is now considered unsound. The coach must stay with those exercises that are event specific throughout the training year.

The changes to overcome adaptation and boredom are done through altering the number of reps and sets. Researchers have found that it is necessary for an exercise to be used for a period of five to six months for maximum results in strength and hypertrophy. So don't change exercises; change the reps and sets.

It is imperative to continue the same exercises throughout the whole macrocycle for maximum results. For this reason, the coach must carefully study all the exercises that are available and decide which ones would be most beneficial for the specific event.

The *order* in which the athlete does his exercises is also important for maximum benefit. All throwing should be done before weight training, unless there is adequate time for recovery between exercise sessions. This would entail more than one training session a day, which is standard on the elite level where athletes train two to three times a day.

All speed-oriented exercises, such as the Olympic lifts, should be done first, followed by the smaller muscle group exercises of the upper body. Then the exercises of the back, legs and abdomen are performed. When working with weights at extremely high intensity, the exercises for the muscle groups should be alternated to give the muscles rest.

SELECTING STRENGTH TRAINING PROGRAM ELEMENTS

Some coaches study the various journals that detail the training programs of elite athletes and attempt to use them for their own athletes. As we've said, this can be a serious mistake. The coach must understand that the program is designed for that athlete and his specific needs only. Each athlete has his own qualifying circumstances that have a bearing on his training program. To mimic someone else's program may be very harmful to the young athlete. Study other programs, yes, but use ideas from them carefully.

The following information will not present any clear prescriptions, only suggestions that have been used successfully and could be incorporated into your own training program.

The first thing that the coach must do is determine which exercises are helpful for specific events—what exercises would benefit the extensor muscles of the upper and lower body, the trunk muscles, or the development of explosive power.

The coach must be careful to understand what each exercise is supposed to do. For example, there have been electrical-myographic studies done on the incline bench press, which is believed to be a good exercise for the shot put. It was found that this exercise is really a "useless" activity except maybe for bodybuilding. For shot putting, there is no neuromuscular carry-over. The flat bench, however, is almost the exact angle of the arm strike and is, therefore, beneficial.

Another exercise to consider is the squat. How deep does an athlete get when in the power position of *any* throwing event? Is it really necessary for an athlete to do deep squats? Study the position of the athlete in the power position and you will see that the athlete is in a good "athletic" position with an angle of 110 to 115 degrees in the knee joint. For training purposes, most elite throwers will do parallel squats during the preparation phase, but during the competition phase do only half and quarter squats, not only because of the above reason, but also because of the short acceleration and deceleration paths as mentioned earlier. This is a very controversial topic and there are those who dispute this reasoning. Remember, there are many roads to Rome!

Hopefully, the reader understands that the coach must research the lifts he plans for his athletes to use. It is up to the coach to determine what his particular athlete needs for total development. Remember, try not to leave anything to chance!

All exercises must have a purpose. If the exercise does not have any carry-over to a specific event, then don't do it.

THE ZACIORSKIY TABLE

When developing a strength training program, it is helpful for the coach to use the Zaciorskiy Table for determining what percentages the athlete should use when following the program prescribed by the coach. Zaciorskiy developed this table based on the percentage of weight to be used in relation to the number of repetitions. His studies indicate that doing fewer repetitions than called for in the table results in no neuromuscular stimulation for the development of strength.

The Zaciorskiy Table		
Repetitions	**Percentage**	**Revised Version(G. Dunn)**
1	100%	100%
2-3	95%	97%
4	90%	95%
5	85%	90%
6	80%	85%
7	75%	80%
8	70%	77%
9	65%	75%
10	60%	70%

From V.M. Zaciorskiy, "Die Körperlichen Eigenschaften des Sportlers" (trans. from Russian). In *Theorie und Praxis des Körperkultur 20* (1971), Special Issue 2.

The table is based on a 1 Rep Max to determine how much weight to use for any specific number of repetitions.

The Revised Version is only an advanced version for an athlete capable of working with heavier intensities. For the average high school athlete, the original table is adequate until he has a good basic training age of two to three years.

We know that to get maximum strength development, the athlete must lift in the range of 80% to 100%. Along with this, it has been found that it's not the speed of the contraction, but the force of the contraction that determines the selection of either slow-twitch or fast-twitch muscle fibers. So, the greater the force working with very intense loads of the contraction of the muscle fibers, the better the athlete is able to develop his fast-twitch fibers. This is all very important, because throwers depend upon explosive power for maximum speed release of the implement.

When involved in heavy, intense training (90% to 100%), the athlete should alternate days of medium and low training. This is necessary for the purpose of recovery and the prevention of overtraining.

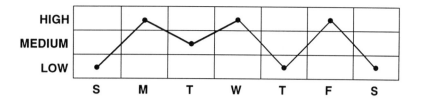

The coach, again, must be sure that each exercise is used a minimum of twice a week. The program can be set up in different ways. The lifting can take place three, four and six time a week. If four or six times a week, a split routine is used: upper body work on two or three days and lower body work on the other two or three days within the week. In many high schools, weight training has become an integral part of the physical education program. This enables the athlete to lift twice a day. He may set up his program so that he does his Olympic lifts during P.E. class and the rest of his lifting after he has completed his technique work during practice.

There are many ways that the weight training program schedule can be changed. Variety in exercises may not be acceptable, but variety in the number of sets or reps is acceptable. Following is an example of a basic program for the freshman or sophomore in high school.

November	4 x 10	(65%)	March	4 x 6	(80%)
December	5 x 7	(75%)	April	5 x 5	(85%)
January	4 x 5	(85%)	May	4 x 2-3	(95%)
February	5 x 4	(90%)	June	5 x 8	(70%)

An example of a high intensity program that could be used by an advanced athlete would be *Load Leaping*.

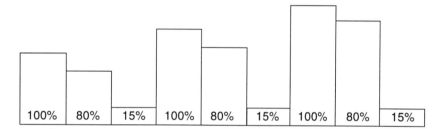

The coach can use any rep and set combination he wants, but note that there is an increase in the volume, not the intensity of each cycle. Each cycle lasts three week (mesocycles). Below are three different programs of "load leaping" to demonstrate how variety can be added to the strength program. This method of training should be used only by advanced athletes, never with high school athletes unless they have had a good basic background during their freshman through junior years.)

	1st Cycle	2nd Cycle	3rd Cycle
Wk 1	4 x 5	5 x 5	6 x 5
Wk 2	3 x 5	4 x 5	5 x 5
Wk 3	PR	PR	PR
Wk1	5 x 3	6 x 3	7 x 3
Wk2	4 x 3	5 x 3	6 x 3
	PR	PR	PR
Wk1	5+4+3+2+1	6+5+4+3+2+1	7+6+5+4+3+2+1
Wk2	4+3+2+1	5+4+3+2+1	6+5+4+3+2+1
Wk3	PR	PR	PR

Most mesocycles are three to four weeks long. If the coach changes the rep-set routine of each mesocycle, his athletes will experience no boredom or plateauing.

A very important study has found that for throwers, in terms of explosive power, the most important type of strength training is with maximal contractions. But to develop hyperthrophy or muscle mass, the athlete must do sub-max training. Doing sub-max training for long periods of time has a negative effect on the fast-twitch fibers of the neuromuscular system.

Therefore, if the athlete's season starts in January, then it is important to alternate sub-max and max training during each mesocycle of the preparatory phase. Then during the last mesocycle before the competitive phase, sub-max and max training are alternated every microcycle. During the competitive phase, only max training is used. Even during the performance of an exercise, sub-max and max training can be done by using the Mixed Method.

For those athletes who start in September or November, the following schedule could be used:

September — Sub-Max
October — Sub-Max
November — Max
December — Sub-Max
January — Alternate Sub-Max and Max every microcycle
February — Eccentric/Concentric combinations
March — Using Mixed Method (Sub-Max & Max during the performance of the exercise, i.e., Pyramids.)
April — Max
May — Max

Those starting in March must do Max training as soon as possible, because at this time, it is too late to attempt to develop hypertrophy.

The last week in each mesocycle can be used to determine new personal records for the different exercises. When going for new maximums, it must be noted that if the attempts fail to reach the previous maximum, the athlete must adjust to the new max, even though it is lower than the previous standard. The training of the athlete must be adjusted to how he feels because there are many factors that can affect this critical element: recent illness, long hours of studying for an exam, family problems, and the like.

SPECIFIC STRENGTH TRAINING

Another very important aspect of strength training is specific weight training. These are exercises that are specific to the event, using barbells or plates. An example of a shot put specific exercise is the *Tossing Clean*. The athlete cleans the bar to the chest position and, with as little hesitation as possible, tosses the bar out in front of him into an old high jump pit.

A modification of the same exercise is the *Sitting Tossing Clean*. The athlete sits on an 18" box. He is handed a barbell by two training partners. He stands and tosses the bar into the high jump pit. The athlete must be as explosive as possible. These exercises can replace regular, upper body barbell exercises or can be used in conjunction with the Olympic lifts. These are usually done in six to ten sets of three to five repetitions at 60% to 80% of the athlete's clean max.

Another specific exercise is *Tossing the Plate*. The athlete stands in a modified power position, the shoulders are turned to the four o'clock position and the lay-back is not very deep. He holds a 25- to 35-pound plate against the side of his head with his elbow down and does a standing put. He does eight to ten sets of five repetitions. Again, this exercise can replace an upper body exercise in the weight room.

Another exercise uses a barbell plate weighing 45 to 50 pounds. The athlete assumes a squatting position, holding the barbell plate in the chest pass position. The athlete then drives upward and pushes the weight either straight up or out as directed by the coach.

SPECIAL STRENGTH TRAINING

The use of variable weight implements—as a key to real progress—has become an integral part of the training of all world class throwers.

There are two reasons why this is so. First, it has been found that if the athlete throws the same weight implement day after day, week after week, month after month, the same effects occurs in the neuromuscular system as it does when the same amount of weight is used in weight training every day. There is a plateauing effect; the neuromuscular system adapts to the same old stimulus, resulting in no more improvement.

The second reason is the need to improve some particular aspect. For example, the athlete may need to improve his arm speed via the use of lighter implements or he may want to improve specific strength and use an overweight implement.

Individual needs, then, determine which implements to use. It has been found that during the preparation phase, light implements are effective when working on technique, especially for the novice thrower who usually has difficulty learning proper technique because he lacks strength and balance.

Generally, an athlete who needs faster arm speed should concentrate on light implement work, though he should intersperse standard implement workouts in his routine. However, there are some elite athletes who testify that working with the overweight implement has a more positive effect on their arm speed because of the special strength development. Obviously, the coach must have a real handle on the specific needs of the individual athlete and how he responds to the different stimuli.

In some events, such as the javelin, the coach must prepare a schedule that is ordered for positive effect and injury prevention. The use of the lighter implement before the heavy implement is necessary so that the carry-over of the nerve response of the previous throw is still "remembered" by the neuromuscular system. This makes it necessary for the time between each throw of a particular set to be no longer than a few seconds. This type of training is not a technique session, so all throws must be all-out and very explosive.

How heavy should the implement be in these workouts? It has been found that for the shot, discus and hammer, the weight should not exceed or be less than the standard implement by more than two pounds. Research has shown that there is neurological altering of technique if the weight of the implement is either *too* light or *too* heavy.

On the other hand, for standing throws, it is okay to use even heavier (or lighter) implements because there is no danger to the timing of the complete throw. This is another method of special strength development.

The following chart shows how to use the different weight implements in sets. Whether the athlete needs work on speed or strength or just a means of preventing a plateauing effect in the neuromuscular system, the coach must remember that the lighter implement should always be thrown first, followed by the standard and then the overweight implement to complete the set.

Another very important consideration when throwing variable weights is that the athlete must throw the next implement as soon as possible. There should not be any delay between throws. The energy developed in the neuromuscular system when the lighter implement is thrown is still present and the use of the heavier implement "fakes" out the nervous system. This enables the athlete to throw with a higher rate of speed with the heavier implement. The athlete must be rested before the start of the next set—at least five minutes.

NEED	LIGHT	STANDARD	OVERWEIGHT
SPEED	2	1	1
REGULAR	1	2	1
POWER	1	1	2
SPEED & POWER	2	0	2

The coach must control the work. Don't let the athlete get sloppy. Emphasis must be on speed or power. As soon as the technique begins to break down, discontinue the throwing. Always work in sets, with a small number of throws. The throws must be performed with all-out effort. It is advisable that on the days when this program is used, the weight training schedule be either medium, light, or none at all. Studies indicate that recuperation from the variable weight throw workouts is faster than from general weight training workouts, but when they are combined with a heavy training session, the fatigue to the neuromuscular system is too high for complete overnight recuperation.

PLYOMETRICS

The coach and athlete should include in the total training schedule all types of jumps, bounds and specific types of exercises for the development of explosive power and strength. The ability to develop explosive power depends on the speed of the stretch-reflex cycle of the contracting muscle system. In essence, this is training for speed-strength. Researchers have found that it requires special motor training, which is commonly called "plyometric training."

Physiologically, when the athlete lands in the center of the circle after the glide, the muscles are "loaded up" in what is called an eccentric contraction. The same thing is true when the left leg is used in "blocking" for the javelin, discus, and shot.

It is during this eccentric contraction that the muscles are pre-stretched. When the athlete continues from the power position to the release phase, the extensor muscles are in a concentric contraction. The "secret" for maximum results is how quickly the muscles go from eccentric to concentric contraction. The phase between the two contractions is called the *amortization phase*. The shorter this phase, the more explosive the concentric contraction and the greater the force exerted. This is where plyometric exercises come in.

There has been a lot of scientific experimentation done in regard to plyometric training. And there have been many changes in opinion regarding what it is supposed to accomplish. Does the coach want to develop the stretch-reflex (explosive power) or muscle endurance? Probably both!

The coach must be careful how he schedules plyometric training in the macrocycle. It may be necessary to develop "endurance" at the beginning of the macrocycle and then concentrate on developing the stretch-reflex during the competitive phase. At the start of the preparatory phase, the volume should be low and gradually build to a very high level for endurance and then decrease gradually to a low maintenance level of only stretch-reflex exercises until the championship meets.

There are certain guidelines that must be taken into consideration when putting plyometrics into the training schedule. For one thing, they should be done only two times a week. The exercises used should be *low impact* exercises until the athlete can handle the more advanced ones.

The coach should be sure that, when the athlete is doing these exercises, there is a quick response off the ground. When doing low impact exercises of inplace jumps, the athlete should attempt to do them as quickly and as "lightly" as possible. If the athlete has a sluggish response and the feet are "pounding" the ground, this indicates that the athlete does not possess enough strength to do the exercises properly. This is common with novice athletes who have no leg strength and may be overweight. It is recommended that novices do only double leg work until they have sufficient leg strength to prevent possible injury.

There is also the recommendation from the former East German coaches that the athlete be capable of squatting double his body weight before attempting to do depth jumps. But we have found from experience, that if the athlete starts doing depth jumps from as low as a twelve-inch box, he is able to handle that height. If the heel touches the ground at that height, then even twelve-inches is too high. The coach must watch the response of the athlete closely, to determine if the drills are doing him any good.

Another aspect of plyometric training that has to be considered is the need for sufficient rest between sets. If the emphasis is on endurance, then the rest does not have to be long. Even the number of sets can be higher.

But, if the emphasis is on stretch-reflex, then the rest between sets has to be ten minutes or longer. In fact, it is recommended with depth jumps that the "ideal" arrangement would be to do a set in the morning, the second set at noon and the third set in the afternoon before practice. It must be understood that the nervous system needs to be rested as much as possible before the next set for a positive response.

The coach should watch his athletes closely for proper technique when they do plyometrics. When doing depth jumps, the heel must not touch the ground. If it does, the exercise is too difficult and the height is excessive.

Even when ground contact is "too long," there is a negative response. Contact must be quick and light, but not so quick or light that the athlete does not get maximum explosion.

The use of force plates is an excellent means to determine if the athlete is getting proper response from each jump. (Force plates can be purchased at a reasonable price.) Otherwise the coach must observe his athlete closely to "eye-ball" good consistent reactions or use the results of various measurements, such as vertical jumps, standing long jumps, consecutive jumps or hops, etc. The coach should record this information for future reference and to develop a model to help determine or predict potential throwers.

The landing surface cannot be so soft that it yields too much. If it is, the athlete does not get proper response from the ground and thus cannot achieve the desired training effect.

Because all plyometric drills primarily work on the nervous system, it is recommended that the athlete not add a lot of extra weight, such as a weight vest, when performing the jumps. It has been found that even a relatively small weight leads to premature fatigue to the nervous system and thus reduces the effectiveness of the exercise.

Using hops, jumps from the ground, jumps off a box, and so on, the coach must realize that the extension of the legs on the rebound after a jump or hop is very similar to the extension of the leg and foot during each of the throwing events. This is why many feel the use of plyometric drills must be an integral part of the training program.

There are two types of plyometric exercises: general and specific. The general exercises include those that involve hops and jumps, and the specific exercises are event specific.

There are many booklets, videotapes, and articles on plyometrics, and the coach and athlete are encouraged to research these so that they have a good catalog of the different types and kinds of jumps available to them for the training schedule. Vern Gambetta, a sports consultant and former editor of *Track Technique*, has classified them into Inplace Jumps, Short Response Jumps, and Long Response Exercises. Below are brief samples of the different categories. A coach can develop a very large list of useful exercises.

GENERAL PLYOMETRIC EXERCISES (USED IN ALL SPORTS)

From Vern Gambetta, Plyometrics, National Strength and Conditioning Assn., 300 Old City Hall Landmark, 920 O Street, Lincoln, NE 68508.

Low Impact Exercises

Inplace	Short Response	Long Response
Ankle Hops	Standing Long Jump	Bounding Skips
Tuck Jumps		
Split Jumps		
Lateral Bounce		
Ice Skater		
Spin Jumps		
Lateral Cone Jump		

Intermediate Impact Exercises

Cycle Jumps	3 x Standing Long Jump	10 x Bound
Cycle Jump-Butt Kick	Standing Triple Jump	
Drop Jump (18" Box)	Single Hurdle Hop	
Jump Ups (18" Box)	Ski	
Lateral Hops	Zig-Zag Bounce	
	Crossover Bounce	
	5 x Single-Leg Hop	
	5 x Bound (High)	

High Impact Exercises

High Single-Leg Hops	5 x Standing Long Jump	10 x Single-Leg Hops
	Double-Leg Box Jumps	Hop and Step
	10 x Hurdle Rebounds	(2 each)
	5 x Double-Leg Hops	Speed Bounding
	(Go for it)	

Shock Jumps

Step off 18" box and do vertical jump
Step off 18" box and over hurdle
Step off 18" box up to another 18" box
Step off 18" box standing long jump
Single leg hops over mini-hurdles
Bounding onto a series of 18" boxes (Triple Jump Drills)

Shoulder Plyo's

Alternate arm pushups using medicine ball
Drop pushups from 12" gynmastic pads
Drop and rebound pushups from 12" gymnastic pads

SPECIFIC PLYOMETRIC EXERCISES

The Shot Box

Specific plyometric exercises imitate the event. One is called the Shot Box. The 12"-high box is placed in the back of the shot put circle. The athlete assumes the same position that he does in the back of the circle, except that he is standing on the 12" box from which he does the complete shot put technique.

The essential aspect of the drill is that the athlete lands in the power position and immediately drives the shot put. There cannot be any settling or pause. The critical point of all plyometric drills is the immediate rebound or the shortest possible amortization phase between eccentric and concentric contractions. The same drill can be used for discus and javelin as well.

The Pendulum Shot

An overweight shot of 22 pounds or more is attached to the end of a 16-foot pipe suspended from the ceiling. The athlete, standing in the final shot put release position, swings the shot out of his left hand. As it swings back, he catches it in his outstretched right hand and when the shot gets to the neck, he immediately punches the shot back in the normal shot put action. Again, the critical point is the immediate rebound of the shot, the shortest possible amortization phase possible. This drill can also be used for the discus and javelin.

Sergio Zanon of Italy, the original designer of these exercises, recommends that five to eight repetitions and six to ten sets of the exercises be performed in a training unit with 10-15 minutes rest between sets. To increase the intensity of the exercise, the athlete increases the arc of the swing, not the weight of the implement. Remember, it's the switching from the eccentric to the concentric contractions that makes this exercise beneficial to the athlete. He must work to reduce the amortization phase. It is here that maximum force is developed, because the rate of stretch is more important than the magnitude.

Specific plyometric exercises should be discontinued ten days before important competitions. The intensity must follow an undulatory course with a frequency of about 20 days.

FLEXIBILITY AND BALANCE

Included in this group of exercises is mobility as well. Accelerating the implement through as long a path as possible requires flexibility, mobility and balance. In many cases, the novice thrower is a large athlete and is often lacking in one or all of these very important factors that make a good athlete.

Mobility can often be improved by participation in such activities as basketball, soccer, wrestling, football, etc.—activities that require body control. Gymnastics exercises on the tumbling mat are very good but just doing the very basic tumbling skills of forward and backward rolls can be difficult for large athletes.

There are many tumbling skills that the coach can use to help improve the mobility of his athletes, and they can be a lot of fun. The use of gymnastics equipment, such as the horse, parallel bars and rings can be very challenging to the big athlete and sometimes very difficult.

The trampoline is an excellent apparatus to use for mobility. There are many drills that can be done on the trampoline that are very similar to the event itself. This piece of apparatus is hard to come by because of the high risk factor, but if there is proper supervision and spotting, its use can be safe and beneficial to the athlete.

A series of mobility exercises can be used as part of the sprint program. The coach can have the athlete assume different positions from which he must move as quickly as possible into a sprinting position. The athlete could lie on his back or stomach, or he could be on his hands and knees facing a different direction. Having athletes compete against each other from these positions can make these drills even more meaningful. Always use a stopwatch. Flexibility exercises must be an integral part of the athlete's training program for him to be able to assume the sound biomechanical positions of the events.

The following flexibility exercises can be used in most of the throwing events. Obviously, some are more event specific, and the coach and athlete have to select those that will benefit him the most.

From Max Jones, *Throwing*, Ramsbury: British Amateur Athletic Board, 1987

147

BALANCE DRILLS

An area of training that many coaches are not aware of today is the use of balance drills. Coach Vern Gambetta and Lois Klatt of Concordia College have done extensive research on specific stabilization strength and its relationship to athletic efficiency and the reduction of athletic injuries.

They have concluded that stabilization strength or balance has to be a part of every training program, for the advanced athlete as well as the novice. Statistics bear them out. The obvious need for balance is critical in all sports, but few coaches will spend time training their athletes in this area.

Bob Gajda, in his book, *Total Body Training*, describes two types of balance training using two pieces of equipment that can be easily made and should be used by all serious throwers.

THE O-BEAM

The first piece of apparatus is called the "O-Beam" (Oscillating Beam). This beam is 3 inches wide on one side and $3^1/_2$ inches on the other side. It is 12 to 14 feet long, beveled 1/2 inch on each corner. This beveling takes away the stability when it lays flat on the floor and requires the athlete to do more to stay on the beam. The drills become more difficult when using the narrower side.

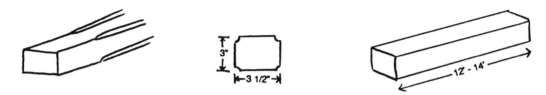

The athlete performs the exercises barefooted so that his feet have complete sensory feeling. Various suggested exercises follow.

Beginning Skills

- Walking forward and backward
- Quarter squats on one leg while leaning forward or in a sitting position
- Toe raises on two legs, in sideways position
- Walk, pivot, walk
- Walk on toes
- Swing step, move free leg along side the beam by depressing the hips.

Intermediate Skills

- Walk quickly
- Side shuffle
- Hop
- All fours
- Stork stand (hip flexed, on one leg)
- Command touch—move hand to spot named by a partner
- Balance touch—touch an object on the floor with free leg while maintaining balance
- Toe raise, on one leg, in side position
- Lunge.

Advanced Skills

- Heel-toe walk
- Cross over (in front), moving sideways
- Cross over (behind), moving backwards
- Walk on all fours

- Walk quickly backward
- Hop with quarter turns
- Hop sideways
- Lunge, jump up, return to lunge position
- Lunge, jump, switch lead leg
- Lateral squat-attempt to touch fingers of hands clasped behind back of head
- Walk on all fours, then lift leg off beam. Secure balance and position
- Thread-step through clasped hands and return.

Very Skilled

- Burst forward and stop
- Lunge, jump, half-turn to lunge with same leg leading
- Lunge, jump, half-turn to lunge with opposite leg leading
- Hop, half-turn
- Jump up and land on beam
- Hop backward
- Heel click, return
- Heel slap, return
- Back lever (free leg extended), full squat, and return.

There are many other drills that should be used, drills that are sport-specific, such as doing the shot put glide and even finishing up with the complete throw. Try a discus or shot put spin turn on the "O-Beam" for a real challenge.

THE K-BOARD

Another very innovative piece of equipment is the "K-Board" (Kinesthetic Primer Board). It is a board that is 18 inches square and 3/4-inch thick. On the bottom is a board that is 18 inches long, $2^1/2$ inches wide and 3/4-inch thick.

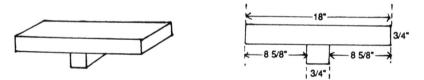

The athlete stands on the board one of two ways: with his feet perpendicular to the bottom board, so that he can rock either frontward or backward, or with his feet parallel to the bottom board, so that he can rock either to the left or to the right. The following exercises can be done on the K-Board:

- Erect standing, front to back
- Erect standing, side to side
- Squatting, front to back
- Single-leg, standing, front to back
- Single-leg, standing, side to side (foot is positioned in the center).

Many of the single-support plyometric drills require stability strength of the ankle and knee joints, making balance a perfect early and continuing preparatation phase training tool. Because balance is such a critical factor in the throwing events, anything that the coach can include to develop balance should be in the training schedule.

RUNNING

The last component is running. The most beneficial type for the thrower is anaerobic or short sprints of 15 to 100 meters. As in plyometrics, sprints are very similar to the extension of the legs during the throws.

For example, the plantar flexion of the foot is the same as that of the left foot in the shot put, the left foot from the back of the circle in the discus, the extension of both feet at the release of the hammer. Sprints are very dynamic and an excellent training component for the throws.

Aerobic or endurance running can also be beneficial. First, aerobic running enhances the endurance indices of the other components; in other words, the athlete can train longer without tiring. Second, it can also be used as a means of weight control. The elite throwers of today are more on the lean side and are very athletic looking. This has a lot to do with the type of training they are doing today. Excess weight can have a negative effect on performance.

SAMPLE YEARLY TRAINING SCHEDULE (MACROCYCLE)

NOVEMBER

TECHNIQUE:	700 throws for the month. Five day a week. Light — 70%, Standard — 30%, Imitations — 350.
STRENGTH:	5 x 8-10 (80%). Partner help with last reps. Three days a week.
PLYOMETRICS:	500 touches a month. Double-leg and single hops, no boxes. Two days a week.
MEDICINE BALL:	100 per week. Two days a week.
MOBILITY:	Tumbling, gymnastics, "O" Beam, etc. Two days per week.
RUNNING:	800 meters before and after practice. Sprints of 50 to 100 meters. 1600-meter endurance runs. Two days a week.

DECEMBER

TECHNIQUE:	800 throws for the month. Five days per week. Light — 60%, Standard — 30%, Overweight — 10%, Imitations — 350.
STRENGTH:	5 x 8 (85-95%). Partner helps with last reps. Three days a week. Use other bodybuilding methods: supersets, negatives, etc.
PLYOMETRICS:	600 touches a month. Double-leg, boxes, and specific drills: pendulum shot.
MEDICINE BALL:	150 per week. two days a week.
MOBILITY:	Tumbling, gymnastics, basketball, "O" Beam, hurdle running.
RUNNING:	50- to 150-meter sprints, agility sprints, 800 meters before and after practice, 1600-meter endurance runs two days a week.

JANUARY

TECHNIQUE:	900/1000 throws for the month. Six days a week. Two days a week, variable training: Variable (according to athlete's needs); 10 x (2+1+1) speed work or 10 x (1+2+1) regular work or 10 x (1+1+2) strength. Four days a week: Standard — 40%, Overweight — 60%.
STRENGTH:	7 x 80%, 5 x 85%, 3 x 90%, 2 x 95%, 1 x 100%, 3 x 95%, 7 x 85%. Partner help for last reps. Specific strength: Tossing cleans, standing throws with barbell plates, etc.
PLYOMETRICS:	800 touches a month. Double-leg hops, single-leg hops, hurdle hops, boxes, etc. Specific plyo's: pendulum shot, shot box, etc.
MEDICINE BALL:	200 throws for week. Two days per week.
MOBILITY:	Tumbling, gymnastics, basketball, running hurdles. Two days per week.
RUNNING:	Sprints from blocks, agility sprints x 15-30 meters, 800 meters before and after every practice.

FEBRUARY (Indoor Meets)

TECHNIQUE:	700 throws. Six days a week. Variable (according to athlete's needs); 10 x (2+1+1) speed work or 10 x (1+2+1) regular work or 10 x (1+1+2) strength for

	three days. Other days: Light — 30%, Standard — 30%, Overweight — 40%.
STRENGTH:	6 x 80%, 4 x 90%, 3 x 95%, 4 x 90%, 5 x 85%. Specific strength: Tossing cleans, throwing barbell plates from various positions: overhead, sideways, forward, etc.
PLYOMETRICS:	1000-1200 touches for the month. Double-leg and single-leg hops of boxes, hurdle hops, depth jumps. Shot box (60-80 per week). Pendulum shot (70-80 per week).
MEDICINE BALL:	200 throws for the week. Two days per week.
MOBILITY:	Run hurdles, basketball, practice long jump and triple jump.
RUNNING:	Sprints from blocks, agility sprints. Two days per week. 800 meters before each practice.

MARCH

TECHNIQUE:	900-1000 throws for the month. Six days a week. Variable: 10 x (2+1+1) speed or 10 x (1+2+1) regular or 10 x (1+1+2) strength. Three days a week. Imitations — 300-400 per week.
STRENGTH:	6 x 82%, 5 x 85%, 5 x 88%, 5 x 85%, 6 x 82%. Three days a week. Combined eccentric and concentric routines, etc.
PLYOMETRICS:	800 touches per month. Double and single-leg hops using boxes, depth jumps, hurdle hops. Shot box (80-100 per week). Pendulum shot (70-80 per week).
MOBILITY:	Run hurdles, long and triple jumps, basketball, racquetball.
RUNNING:	800 meters before practice. Sprints from blocks, flying starts, agility sprints. Two days per week. 10 per week.

APRIL (Outdoor Season)

TECHNIQUE:	800 throws for the month. Six days a week. Mix throws according to athletes needs: 10 x (3+2) (standard+overweight) or 10 x (3+2) (light+overweight) or 10 x (2+3) (standard+overweight) or 10 x (3+2) (light+standard). Imitations — 300 to 400 per week.
STRENGTH:	5 x 85%, 4 x 90%, 3 x 95%, 2 x 97%, 1 x 100%. Three times a week.
PLYOMETRICS:	600 touches a week. Double- and single-leg hops, depth jumps, hurdle hops, shot box and pendulum shot.
MOBILITY:	Run hurdles, long and triple jumps. Two days per week.
RUNNING:	800 meters before each practice and competition. Sprints from blocks x 4-6. Two days per week.

MAY (Peaking for the State Meet)

SECOND WEEK — CONFERENCE MEET

TECHNIQUE:	Depending upon the athlete's needs, use either light, standard or overweight implements. 30 to 40 throws a day.
STRENGTH:	5 x 85%, 4 x 90%, 3 x 95%, 2 x 97%, 1 x 100%. Two times a week. Tuesday and Friday. Snatch, Bench and 1/2 to 1/4 Squats.
PLYOMETRICS:	Hurdle hops 4-5 x 10. Max Jones Test (Test is in back of this manual.)
RUNNING:	800 meters before practice and meet. 3 x 30 sprints on Wednesday.

THIRD WEEK — SECTIONAL MEET

TECHNIQUE:	Emphasis is on speed of release. 20-30 throws a day.
STRENGTH:	5 x 85%, 3 x 90%, 2 x 95%, 1 x 100%. Two days. Tuesday and Friday. Snatch, Bench and 1/2-1/4 squats.

PLYOMETRICS:	Hurdle Hops 4 x 10. Monday and Wednesday.
MOBILITY:	Run hurdles, racquetball. One day this week.
RUNNING:	800 meters before practice and meet. 3 x 30m standing sprints. Monday and Wednesday.

FOURTH WEEK — STATE MEET

TECHNIQUE:	Monday — 8 x 5 (Overweight). Imitations for 20 minutes.
	Tuesday — 2 x 10 (Standard). Concentrate on technique — 60% to 80% of PR.
	Wednesday — No throwing.
	Thursday — 2 x (3+2) (Light+Overweight)
	Friday—State Prelims
	Saturday—State Finals
STRENGTH:	Monday — Snatch 2 x 3 (85%), Bench and Squats 5 x 85%, 3 x 90%, 2 x 95%
	Thursday morning — Snatch 2 x 3 (85%). Squats and Bench 5 x 85%, 3 x 90%, 2 x 95%.
PLYOMETRICS:	Hurdle Hops — 4 x 10 Tuesday.
RUNNING:	800m run before every practice and meet

SAMPLE MICROCYCLE TRAINING SCHEDULES

Below are two examples, one of a microcycle during the preparatory phase and the other during the competitive phase.

JANUARY

Monday	800m run
	Discus — 40 throws, including drills and warmups.
	Bench — 6 x 85%, 5 x 90%, 5 x 95%, 5 x 90%, 6 x 85%.
	Squats — same as bench
	Press behind neck — 4 x 5 (85%)
	Shot Put sit-ups — 4 x 10 (10#)

Tuesday	800m run
	Shot put — 45 throws, including drills and warmup.
	Hurdle hops — 3 x 10
	180-degree stadium hops double-leg 1 x 24
	Single-leg stadium hops 1 x 24
	Double-leg stadium hops 3 x 24
	15-meter agility sprints x 5
	Hip Snatch — 5 x 70%, 5 x 75%, 3 x 3 (80%), 3 x 2 (85%), 3 x 3 (75%)
	Jerk — 4 x 5 (85%)
	Lateral Leg Raises — 4 x 10

Wednesday	800m run
	Discus — 40 throws, including drills and warmup.
	Bench — 5 sets of 4 eccentric hooks (100%) + 6 concentric contractions (50%).
	Squats — 5 sets of 6 eccentric hooks (110%) and 6 concentric contractions (60%) followed by 6 squat jumps (60%).
	Press Behind the Neck — 4 x 5 (85%)
	Shot Put Situps — 4 x 10 (10#)

Thursday and Friday are the same as Tuesday and Monday.

APRIL

Monday	800m run Shot Put — 40 throws, including drills and warmup. Hip Snatch — 5 x 70%, 3 x 3 (80%), 3 x 2 (85%), 3 x 1 (90%) Dynamic Bench — 5 x 80%, 4 x 85%, 3 x 90%, 2 x 95%, 1 x 100% 1/2 Squats — same as bench Barbell Twist — 4 x 10 (100%).
Tuesday	800m run Shot Put Competition — 3 stand warmup, 2 glides warmup, 6 throws in competition. Discus — 3 stand warmup, 2 full turn warmup.
Wednesday	800m run Discus — 35 throws, including drills and warmup. Hurdle Hops — 5 x 10 Hip Snatch — 5 x 70%, 3 x 3 (80%), 3 x 2 (85%), 3 x 1 (90%) Dynamic Bench — 5 x 80%, 4 x 85%, 3 x 90%, 2 x 95% 1/2 Squat — same as the bench Shot Put Sit-ups — 4 x 10 (100%).
Thursday	800m run Shot Put — 35 throws, including drills and warmup. Jerk — 5 x 80%, 4 x 85%, 3 x 90%, 2 x 95%, 1 x 100% Dumbbell Flys — 4 x 10 (100%) Crunches — 1 x 20.
Friday	800m run Discus — 45 throws, including drills and warmup. Hurdle Hops — 5 x 10 Hip Snatch — 5 x 70%, 3 x 3 (80%), 3 x 2 (85%), 3 x 1 (90%) Dynamic Bench — 5 x 80%, 4 x 85%, 3 90%, 2 x 95%, 1 x 100% 1/2 Squats — same as bench.
Saturday	800m run Shot Put Competition — 3 stand warmup, 2 glides warmup, 6 throws in competition. Discus — 3 stand warmup, 2 full turn warmup.

(Note) The dynamic bench uses a three inch pad on the chest, on which the bar rebounds off the pad to get quick acceleration of the concentric contraction.

TESTING AND PREDICTING

This is an area that many coaches neglect because they do not keep records. If the coach has kept records over a period of years, he will have developed norms that will give him feedback on the potential of the athletes tested.

There are simple tests that the high school coach can use to determine if any of his students have the potential to be good throwers. One of the most common tests in use today is the American Association of Health, Physical Education and Recreation test that is used in physical education classes all over the country. Any student who scores in the 80th to 85th percentile is a better than average student. A freshman who can do an eight-foot standing long jump has the potential to be a state champion. It's even more promising if he has good height and size.

Another good predictor is the vertical jump. If a freshman is able to jump 20 inches or more, he is an excellent candidate for the state meet.

In terms of strength, it has been found that if an athlete possesses the following strength components, he is capable of doing well on the state championship level:

Bench Press	—	400 pounds or more
Full Squat	—	400-500 pounds or more
Power Clean	—	300 pounds or more
Power Snatch	—	220 pounds or more

THE MAX JONES QUADRATHLON

There is another testing instrument developed by Max Jones, a national throws coach for England. It is an excellent means of monitoring the progress of your throwers by testing them once a month. If the athlete's training program is sound and progressive, the Max Jones test should show you how much your athlete is improving each test interval. And if the test is administered two weeks before the state meet, when the athlete is "backing off," it can be a good predictor of success.

If the training program has been working well for the athlete and (most important!) if he has worked hard, there is a dramatic jump in the score. During the year, the scores may increase only a few points and may even drop because of high volume and intensity. But once the volume and intensity are gradually lowered and athletes are rested, the points suddenly increase 30, 40 and even 50 points.

Our experience is that a high school athlete who scores over 300-325 points is ready to perform at a very high level, assuming that his technique, size, weight, etc. are where they should be for a thrower at his level.

The four test items used are very easy to administer and need nothing more than a stopwatch and tape measure. It is a good "easy and fun day" activity. The coach should have only this activity for the day. The test items are as follows:

THREE JUMPS: Feet together, hop three times and land either in a long jump pit or on a flat mat.

STANDING LONG JUMP: Standing at the edge of the long jump pit, with toes slightly over the edge of the pit, the athlete does a standing long jump into the pit.

THIRTY-METER SPRINT: Using starting blocks, the athlete starts on the command of the timer at the finish line. The timer starts the watch when the back foot makes contact with the ground.

OVERHEAD SHOT: The athlete stands on top of the stopboard, swings the shot between the legs then throws the shot overhead backwards. It is not necessary to remain on the stopboard.

TEST QUADRATHLON TABLES (1992)

Points	3 Jumps	S.L.J.	30m	O.H. Shot	Points	3 Jumps	S.L.J.	30m	O.H. Shot
1	3.00	1.00	5.80	4.00	51	7.04	2.36	4.38	12.58
2	3.08	1.02	5.77	4.17	52	7.12	2.39	4.35	12.75
3	3.16	1.05	5.74	4.34	53	7.20	2.41	4.33	12.92
4	3.24	1.08	5.71	4.51	54	7.28	2.44	4.30	13.10
5	3.32	1.10	5.68	4.68	55	7.36	2.47	4.27	13.27
6	3.40	1.13	5.66	4.85	56	7.44	2.50	4.24	13.44
7	3.48	1.16	5.63	5.03	57	7.52	2.52	4.21	13.61
8	3.56	1.19	5.60	5.20	58	7.60	2.55	4.18	13.78
9	3.64	1.21	5.57	5.37	59	7.63	2.58	4.16	13.95
10	3.72	1.24	5.54	5.54	60	7.76	2.60	4.13	14.13
11	3.80	1.27	5.51	5.71	61	7.84	2.63	4.10	14.30
12	3.88	1.30	5.49	5.83	62	7.92	2.66	4.07	14.47
13	3.96	1.32	5.46	6.06	63	8.01	2.69	4.04	14.64
14	4.05	1.35	5.43	6.23	64	8.09	2.71	4.02	14.81
15	4.13	1.38	5.40	6.40	65	8.17	2.74	3.99	14.98
16	4.21	1.40	5.37	6.57	66	8.25	2.77	3.96	15.16
17	4.29	1.43	5.34	6.74	67	8.33	2.80	3.93	15.33
18	4.37	1.46	5.32	6.91	68	8.41	2.82	3.90	15.50
19	4.45	1.49	5.29	7.09	69	8.49	2.85	3.87	15.67
20	4.53	1.51	5.26	7.26	70	8.57	2.88	3.85	15.84
21	4.61	1.54	5.23	7.43	71	8.65	2.90	3.82	16.02
22	4.69	1.57	5.20	7.60	72	8.73	2.93	3.79	16.19
23	4.77	1.60	5.17	7.77	73	8.81	2.96	3.76	16.36
24	4.85	1.62	5.15	7.94	74	8.89	2.99	3.73	16.53
25	4.93	1.65	5.12	8.12	75	8.97	3.01	3.70	16.70
26	5.02	1.68	5.09	8.29	76	9.06	3.04	3.68	16.87
27	5.10	1.70	5.06	8.46	77	9.14	3.07	3.65	17.05
28	5.18	1.73	5.03	8.63	78	9.22	3.10	3.62	17.22
29	5.26	1.76	5.01	8.80	79	9.30	3.12	3.59	17.39
30	5.34	1.79	4.98	8.97	80	9.38	3.15	3.56	17.56
31	5.42	1.81	4.95	9.15	81	9.46	3.18	3.53	17.73
32	5.50	1.84	4.92	9.32	82	9.54	3.20	3.51	17.90
33	5.58	1.87	4.89	9.49	83	9.62	3.23	3.48	18.03
34	5.66	1.90	4.86	9.66	84	9.70	3.26	3.45	18.25
35	5.74	1.92	4.84	9.83	85	9.78	3.29	3.42	18.42
36	5.82	1.95	4.81	10.01	86	9.86	3.31	3.39	18.59
37	5.90	1.98	4.78	10.13	87	9.94	3.34	3.36	18.76
38	5.98	2.00	4.75	10.35	88	10.03	3.37	3.34	18.93
39	6.07	2.03	4.72	10.52	89	10.11	3.40	3.31	19.11
40	6.15	2.06	4.69	10.69	90	10.19	3.42	3.28	19.28
41	6.23	2.09	4.67	10.86	91	10.27	3.45	3.25	19.45
42	6.31	2.11	4.64	11.04	92	10.35	3.48	3.22	19.62
43	6.39	2.14	4.61	11.21	93	10.43	3.50	3.20	19.79
44	6.47	2.17	4.58	11.38	94	10.51	3.53	3.18	19.96
45	6.55	2.20	4.55	11.55	95	10.59	3.56	3.15	20.14
46	6.63	2.22	4.52	11.72	96	10.67	3.59	3.12	20.31
47	6.71	2.25	4.50	11.89	97	10.75	3.61	3.09	20.48
48	6.79	2.28	4.47	12.07	98	10.83	3.64	3.06	20.65
49	6.87	2.30	4.44	12.24	99	10.91	3.67	3.03	20.82
50	6.95	2.33	4.41	12.41	100	11.00	3.70	3.01	21.00

Additional Points

3 Jumps: 1 Point extra for each 8 cms above 11.00   30m: 1 point for each 0.03 below 3.01
S.L.J.:   1 point for each 3 cm above 3.70   O.H. Shot: 1 point for each 7 cm above 21.00

GOOD READING FROM TRACK & FIELD NEWS

THE THROWS: Contemporary Theory, Technique and Training. Jess Jarver, ed. A fine collection of articles and research from world authorities on all aspects of the four throwing events. 136pp. 1994. 4th ed. $16.50

THE DYNAMICS OF THE JAVELIN THROW, Dr. Robert Sing. The most complete and authoritative work on javelin training, technique, common injures, weight training, more. 1984. Profusely illustrated. $20.00

PEAK WHEN IT COUNTS, Dr. William H. Freeman. The first comprehensive treatment of periodized training (or how to peak for the big meets) for the American coach. All event groups covered. 3rd ed., 1996. 136pp. Many tables and figures. $15.95

BASIC TRACK & FIELD BIOMECHANICS, Tom Ecker. The best introduction in understandable language to the concepts of biomechanics and their application to each t&f event. Essential reading for the coach. 160pp. 2nd ed., 1996. Well illustrated. $17.50

THE JUMPS: Contemporary Theory, Technique and Training, Jess Jarver, ed. Another fine collection of articles contributed by world authorities on the high jump, pole vault, long and triple jump. 4th ed. 1994. 126pp. $16.50

ED. FERN'S FLIGHT SCHOOL. Prep coach and former national-class jumper Ed. Fern offers an individual approach to coaching high school high jumpers. 80pp. 1990. $6.00

TRACK COACH (*Formerly "Track Technique"*). The official technical publication of USA Track & Field. Published quarterly by Track & Field News. $20.00 yr. USA

TRACK & FIELD NEWS. "The bible of the sport." All the national and international major meet results, statistical lists and rankings, interviews, profiles, action photos, etc. from high school through the Olympics. Monthly. $38.95 yr. USA